Microsoft® SharePoint® 2010 Configuration (70-667)

Lab Manual

WILEY

EXECUTIVE EDITOR	John Kane
EDITORIAL PROGRAM ASSISTANT	Jennifer Lartz
DIRECTOR OF SALES	Mitchell Beaton
EXECUTIVE MARKETING MANAGER	Chris Ruel
SENIOR PRODUCTION & MANUFACTURING MANAGER	Janis Soo
ASSOCIATE PRODUCTION MANAGER	Joel Balbin

Founded in 1807, John Wiley & Sons, Inc. has been a valued source of knowledge and understanding for more than 200 years, helping people around the world meet their needs and fulfill their aspirations. Our company is built on a foundation of principles that include responsibility to the communities we serve and where we live and work. In 2008, we launched a Corporate Citizenship Initiative, a global effort to address the environmental, social, economic, and ethical challenges we face in our business. Among the issues we are addressing are carbon impact, paper specifications and procurement, ethical conduct within our business and among our vendors, and community and charitable support. For more information, please visit our website: www.wiley.com/go/citizenship.

To order books or for customer service, please call 1-800-CALL WILEY (225-5945).

ISBN 978-0-470-53868-5

Printed in the United States of America

10 9 8 7 6 5 4 3 2 1

BRIEF CONTENTS

CONTENTS

LAB 1
INTRODUCTION TO SHAREPOINT 2010

THIS LAB CONTAINS THE FOLLOWING EXERCISES AND ACTIVITIES:

Exercise 1.1   Install Office 2010 Professional

Exercise 1.2   Create and Manage a Site

Exercise 1.3   Create and Manage a List

Exercise 1.4   Create and Manage a Library

Exercise 1.5   Create and Manage Alerts

BEFORE YOU BEGIN

The lab environment consists of student server connected to a local area network, along with a server that functions as the domain controller for a domain called contoso.com. It is also a SharePoint 2010 server. The computers required for this lab are listed in Table 1-1.

Table1-1
Computers required for Lab 1

Computer	Operating System	Computer Name
Instructor Server	Windows Server 2008 R2	RWDC01
Student Server	Windows Server 2008 R2	Studentxx, where xx is your Student number.

> **NOTE**
> *In a classroom lab or virtual lab environment, there will be one classroom server and the students will have workstations named using consecutive numbers in place of the XX variable.*

In addition to the computers, you will also need the software listed in Table 1-2 in order to complete Lab 1.

Table 1-2
Software required for Lab 1

Software	Location
Office 2010 Professional (x17-75058.exe)	\\rwdc01\download
Lab 1 student worksheet	Lab01_worksheet.rtf (provided by instructor)

Working with Lab Worksheets

Each lab in this manual requires that you answer questions, shoot screen shots, and perform other activities that you will document in a worksheet named for the lab (such as Lab01_worksheet.rtf). Your instructor will provide you with access to the worksheets. It is recommended that you use a USB flash drive to store your worksheets so you can submit them to your instructor for review. As you perform the exercises in each lab, open the appropriate worksheet file using WordPad, fill in the required information, and save the file to your flash drive.

SCENARIO

You were just hired as a new SharePoint administrator and you want to test some of the functionality of the current SharePoint environment. In this lab, you will to log on to the current SharePoint environment, create some sites, create a list, create a document library, and create an alert.

After completing this lab, you will be able to:

- Install Microsoft Office 2010 Professional

- Create and manage a site

- Create and manage a list

- Create and manage a library

- Create and manage alerts

Estimated lab time: 60 minutes

Exercise 1.1	Install Office 2010 Professional
Overview	In the following exercise, you will install Office 2010 Professional.
Completion time	10 minutes

1. On your student server, log in as *contoso\Studentxx* (*xx* represents your student number) and use *Pa$$w0rd* as the password.

2. Click *Start*, and in the *Search programs and files* search box, type *\\RWDC01\Downloads* and then press *Enter*.

3. Double-click the Office 2010 Professional Installation executable (*x17-75058.exe*).

4. If a UAC prompt displays, click *Yes*.

5. On the Enter your Product key page, type the 25 character key. The evaluation key for Office 2010 Professional is *GR29P-GRYQM-R8YQP-8KDG4-72M4Y*. Click *Continue*.

6. When the software license terms display, select the *I accept the terms of this agreement* and then click *Continue*.

7. Click *Install Now*.

8. When Office is installed, click *Close*.

Question 1	*Why is it important for a SharePoint client to have Office 2010 Professional installed?*

Exercise 1.2	Create and Manage a Site
Overview	In the following exercise, you will create and manage a site on the instructor's SharePoint server.
Completion time	15 minutes

1. On your student server, log in as *contoso\Studentxx* (*xx* represents your student number) and use *Pa$$w0rd* as the password.

2. Open Internet Explorer and go to *the http://rwdc01*.

3. Click the *Site Actions* menu and select *New Site*. The New SharePoint Site page displays (see Figure 1-1).

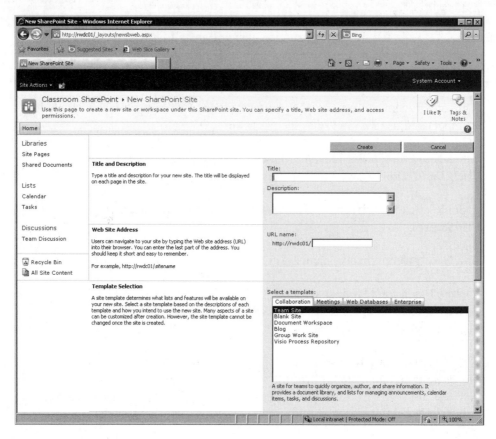

Figure 1-1
The New SharePoint Site page

4. In the *Title* field, type *Student XX Team Site* (*XX* is your student number).

5. For the *URL name* field, type *studentxx* (*xx* is your student number). The entry should read *http://rwdc01/studentXX*.

6. Click *Create*. The *http://rwdc01/StudentXX/SitePages/Home.aspx* Web page displays.

7. On the Ribbon, click the *Page* tab.

8. Click *Edit*.

9. Change *Welcome to your site!* to *Welcome to <Your Name>'s Site!*.

10. On the Ribbon, click *Save & Close*.

11. Open *Site Actions* and select *New Site*. The new SharePoint Site page displays.

12. In the Title field, specify the *Student XX Subsite* (*XX* is your student number).

13. For the *URL name* field, type *subsite1* (*xx* is your student number). The entry should read *http://rwdc01/studentXX/subsite1*.

14. Select the ***Blank Site*** template.

15. Click ***Create***. The ***http://rwdc01/StudentXX/Subsite1/default.aspx*** page displays.

16. Take a screen shot of the message box by pressing Alt+PrtScr and then use Ctrl+V to paste it into your Lab01_worksheet file in the page provided.

17. Click ***Navigate Up*** (see Figure 1-2) and select the ***Student XX*** site.

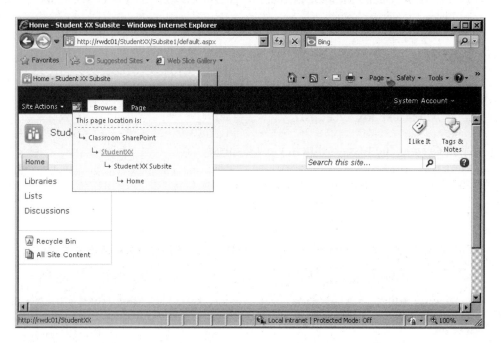

Figure 1-2
Clicking the Navigate Up button

18. Click the Student XX ***Subsite*** link at the top of the page.

19. Open the ***Site Actions*** menu and select ***Site Settings***.

20. In the Site Actions section, click the ***Delete this site*** option.

21. When the Delete This Site page displays, click ***Delete***.

22. When you are prompted to confirm this action, click ***OK***.

23. When the Web site has been deleted, click ***Go back to site***.

24. Go to ***http://rwdc01/StudentXX/SitePages/Home.aspx***.

25. Leave the computer logged on for the next exercise.

Exercise 1.3	Create and Manage a SharePoint List
Overview	In the following exercise, you will create and manage a list on the instructor's SharePoint server.
Completion time	20 minutes

1. On the ***http://rwdc01/StudentXX/SitePages/Home.aspx*** page, click the ***Lists*** option on the vertical bar.

2. At the top of the page, click the ***Create*** option. The Create page displays.

3. Click ***Custom List***. The New page displays.

4. In the ***Name*** text box, type ***List1***.

5. Click ***Create***. The List – All Item view displays.

6. On the Ribbon, in the ***List Tools*** group, click the ***List*** tab.

7. Click ***Create Column*** (see Figure 1-3).

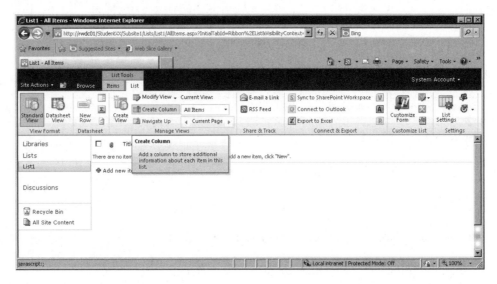

Figure 1-3
Clicking the Create Column option

8. In the ***Column Name*** field, type ***First Name***. Leave the ***Single Line of text*** option selected. Change the maximum number of characters to ***40*** and then click ***OK***.

9. Create a ***Last Name*** column that has a maximum number of characters of ***35*** characters.

10. On the Ribbon, click ***Settings*** and then click ***List Settings***. The List Settings page displays.

11. Click *First Name*.

12. Change the Maximum number of characters to *25* and then click *OK*.

13. Create the following columns by clicking the Create Column link.

     - Name of Company (Single line of text - 40 characters)

     - Job Title (Single line of text - 30 characters)

     - Phone Number (Single line of text - 15 characters)

     - Age (Number)

14. Go to *http://rwdc01/StudentXX/Lists/List1/AllItems.aspx*.

15. Click the *Add new item* option.

16. For the first record, type your information and then click *Save*.

17. Type the data for three additional users.

18. Go back to *http://rwdc01/StudentXX/Lists/List1/AllItems.aspx*.

19. On the Ribbon, in the *List Tools* group, click the *List* option.

20. On the Ribbon, click *Datasheet View*.

21. Type the data for one more person.

22. On the Ribbon, click *Standard View*.

23. To sort by the last name, click the *Last Name* column name.

24. To sort by name of company, click the *Name of Company* column name.

25. On the Ribbon, in the *List Tools* group, click *List*.

26. Click Create *View*. The Create View page displays.

27. Click *Standard View*.

28. In the *Name* text box, type *Basic View*.

29. Make sure that only *First Name*, *Last Name,* and *Phone Number* are selected.

30. Click *OK*.

31. Make sure the Basic View is selected.

32. Take a screen shot of the message box by pressing Alt+PrtScr and then use Ctrl+V to paste it into your Lab01_worksheet file in the page provided.

33. Leave the computer logged on for the next exercise.

Exercise 1.4	Create and Manage a Library
Overview	In the following exercise, you will create and manage a SharePoint Document library.
Completion time	10 minutes

1. On the *http://rwdc01/StudentXX/SitePages/Home.aspx* page, click the *Library* option on the vertical bar. The All Site Content page displays.

2. Click *Create*. The Create page displays.

3. Click *Document Library*.

4. For the name, type *Public Documents*. Click *Create*.

5. Click *Start* and then launch Microsoft Word.

6. If a Welcome dialog box displays, click *Use Recommended Settings* and then click *OK*. If a UAC dialog box displays, click the **Yes** button.

7. Type your name in the Word document and then save it to your desktop as the *Name* document.

8. Close Word.

9. Go back to your document library and click *Add document*. The Upload Document dialog box displays.

10. Click *Browse*. Browse to your desktop and double-click the *Name* document. Click *OK* to upload the document. The Name document should display in the document library.

11. Click to open the context menu for the name document and then select *Edit in Microsoft Word* (see Figure 1-4). Word launches.

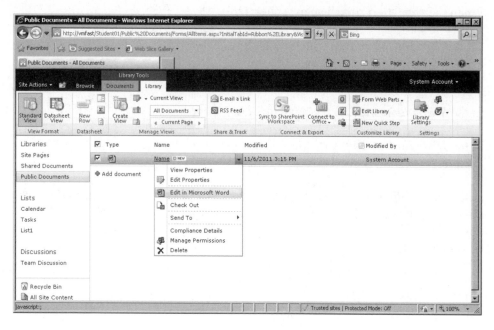

Figure 1-4
Document Library

12. If the document is in Protected View, click the ***Enable Editing*** button at the top
     of the screen.

13. Type the name of your school or the company you work for.

14. Click ***File*** and then click ***Exit***. If you are prompted to save the document, click
     Save.

15. When Word closes, look at the document information displayed in the document
     library and notice the date and the time that the document was modified.

16. Leave the computer logged on for the next exercise.

Exercise 1.5	Create and Manage Alerts
Overview	In the following exercise, you will create and manage alerts in SharePoint.
Completion time	5 minutes

1. Go to ***http://rwdc01/Student01/SitePages/Home.aspx***.

2. On the vertical bar, click ***Public Documents***. The Public Documents document
    library displays.

3. On the Ribbon, in the ***Library Tools*** group, click the ***Library*** tab.

4. Click the ***Alert Me***. When the menu displays, click ***Set Alert on This Library.***

5.   When the *New Alert* page displays, click *OK*.

6.   Click *Alert Me*. When the menu opens, click *Manage My Alerts*.

7.   Open the *Site Actions* menu and select *Site Settings*.

8.   In the *Site Administration* section, click *User Alerts*.

9.   In the *Display alerts for* drop-down, select your user name and then click *Update*.

10. Select the *Public Documents* check box and then click the *Delete Selected Alerts* button. When you are prompted to confirm your selection, click *OK*.

11. Close Internet Explorer.

LAB 2
INSTALLING AND UPGRADING SHAREPOINT 2010 (PART I)

THIS LAB CONTAINS THE FOLLOWING EXERCISES AND ACTIVITIES:

Exercise 2.1   Install SQL Server 2008 Express with Management Console

Exercise 2.2   Install SharePoint 2010 Prerequisites

Exercise 2.3   Install SharePoint 2010 Binaries

Exercise 2.4   Install SharePoint 2010 Service Pack 1

Exercise 2.5   Install the SharePoint 2010 Cumulative Patch

Exercise 2.6   Run the SharePoint 2010 Products Configuration Tool

BEFORE YOU BEGIN

The lab environment consists of student servers connected to a local area network, along with an instructor server that functions as the domain controller, DNS, and Exchange server for a domain called contoso.com. The computers required for this lab are listed in Table 2-1.

Table 2-1
Computers required for Lab 2

Computer	Operating System	Computer Name
Instructor Server	Windows Server 2008 R2	RWDC01
Student Server	Windows Server 2008 R2	Studentxx, where xx is your Student number.

> **NOTE**
> *In a classroom lab or virtual lab environment, there will be one classroom server and the students will have workstations named using consecutive numbers in place of the XX variable.*

In addition to the computers, you will also need the software listed in Table 2-2 in order to complete Lab 2.

Table 2-2
Software required for Lab 2

Software	Location
To Install SQL Server: • Microsoft SQL Server 2008 R2 RTM - Express with Management Tools, SQLEXPRWT_x64_ENU.exe	\\rwdc01\downloads
Microsoft SharePoint 2010 for Enterprise Client Access License	\\rwdc01\downloads
SharePoint Prerequisites: • Windows Identity Foundation (KB974405) Windows6.1-KB974405-x64.msu • Microsoft Sync Framework Runtime v1.0 (x64) SyncSetup_en.x64.zip • Microsoft Chart Controls for Microsoft .NET Framework 3.5 MSChart.exe • Microsoft Filter Pack 2.0 FilterPack64bit.exe • Microsoft SQL Server 2008 Analysis Services ADOMD.NET SQLSERVER2008_ASADOMD10.msi • Microsoft Server Speech Platform Runtime (x64) Platform\x64\SpeechPlatformRuntime.msi • Microsoft Server Speech Recognition Language - TELE(en-US) SR\MSSpeech_SR_en-US_TELE.msi • SQL 2008 R2 Reporting Services SharePoint 2010 Add-in 1033\x64\rsSharePoint.msi • Hotfix for WCF: SharePoint Shared Services Roll-up (Windows6.1-KB976462-v2-x64.msu)	\\rwdc01\downloads
SharePoint 2010 SP1 officeserver2010sp1-kb2460045-x64-fullfile-en-us.exe	\\rwdc01\downloads
Description of the SharePoint Server 2010 cumulative update refresh package (SharePoint server-package): August 30, 2011 office2010kb2553048fullfilex64glb	\\rwdc01\downloads
Lab 2 student worksheet	Lab02_worksheet.rtf (provided by instructor)

Working with Lab Worksheets

Each lab in this manual requires that you answer questions, shoot screen shots, and perform other activities that you will document in a worksheet named for the lab (such as Lab02_worksheet.rtf). Your instructor will provide you with access to the worksheets. It is recommended that you use a USB flash drive to store your worksheets, so you can submit them to your instructor for review. As you perform the exercises in each lab, open the appropriate worksheet file using WordPad, fill in the required information, and save the file to your flash drive.

SCENARIO

As a newly hired administrator, your first task is to install a new SharePoint 2010 environment. To allow SharePoint to be scalable, you will first install SQL Server and then install SharePoint 2010. You will complete this lab by patching SharePoint 2010 by installing Service Pack 1 and a Cumulative Pack.

After completing this lab, you will be able to:

- Install SQL Server 2008 R2

- Install SharePoint 2010

- Install Service Pack 1 and Cumulative Pack

- Run the SharePoint 2010 Products Configuration Program

Estimated lab time: 1 hour 40 minutes

Exercise 2.1	Install SQL Server 2008 Express with Management Console
Overview	In the following exercise, you will install SQL Server 2008 Express with Management Console.
Completion time	20 minutes

Question 1	List at least two reasons why it's best to install a separate SQL server to be used with SharePoint 2010?

1.   On your student server, log in as *contoso\Studentxx* (*xx* represents your student number) and use *Pa$$w0rd* as the password.

2.   Click *Start*, right-click *Computer*, and then click *Manage*.

3.   Click *Features* and then click *Add Features*.

4.   Select *.NET Framework 3.5.1 Features* and then click *Install*.

5.   When you're prompted to add role services, click *Add Required Role Services* and then click *Next*.

6.   When the Introduction to Web Service (IIS) page displays, click *Next*.

7.   When the Select Role Services page displays, click *Next*.

8.   When the Confirm Installation Selections page displays, click *Install*.

9.   When the installation is complete, click *Close*.

10. Click *Start* and in Search Programs and Files search box, type *\\RWDC01\Downloads* and then press *Enter*.

11. Double-click the SQL Server 2008 R2 Express with Management Tools installation file (*SQLEXPRWT_x64_ENU.exe*). The SQL Server Installation Center displays.

12. Click the *New installation or add features to an existing installation* option.

13. On the License Terms page, select the *I accept the license terms* option and then click *Next*.

14. After the setup support files are installed, the Feature Selection page displays. Click *Next*.

15. Select the *Default Instance* option and then click *Next*.

16. The SQL Server service accounts are used to use separate accounts and passwords for each SQL service. Leave the default option selected and then click *Next*.

17. Leave the Windows authentication mode default option selected and then click *Next*.

18. When the Error Reporting page displays, click *Next.*

19. When the installation is complete, take a screen shot of the message box by pressing Alt+PrtScr and then use Ctrl+V to paste it into your Lab02_worksheet file in the page provided.

20. Click **Close**.

Exercise 2.2	Install SharePoint 2010 Prerequisites
Overview	In the following exercise, you will install the SharePoint prerequisites.
Completion time	20 minutes

1. On your student server, log in as *contoso\Studentxx* (*xx* represents your student number) and use *Pa$$w0rd* as the password.

2. Click **Start** and in the **Search programs and files** search box, type *\\RWDC01\Downloads* and then press **Enter**.

3. Double-click the SharePoint executable (*sharepoint.exe*).

4. If the Open File – Security Warning dialog box displays, prompting you to confirm that you want to run the file, click **Yes**.

5. When the Microsoft SharePoint 2010 splash screen displays, click the **Install software prerequisites** option.

6. When the Microsoft SharePoint 2010 Products Preparation Tool wizard begins, click **Next**.

7. When the License Agreement displays, select the **I accept the terms of the License Agreement(s)** check box and then click **Next**.

8. When the prerequisites are installed, click **Finish** and then reboot Windows.

Note: Since the prerequisite installer downloads components from the Microsoft Download Center, you must have Internet access on the computer. If you do not have Internet access, you must manually install each of prerequisite. The prerequisites are located in the \\rwdc01\download folder. This includes:

•   Windows Identity Foundation (KB974405) Windows6.1-KB974405-x64.msu

•   Microsoft Sync Framework Runtime v1.0 (x64) SyncSetup_en.x64.zip

•   Microsoft Chart Controls for Microsoft .NET Framework 3.5 MSChart.exe

•   Microsoft Filter Pack 2.0 FilterPack64bit.exe

- Microsoft SQL Server 2008 Analysis Services ADOMD.NET
  SQLSERVER2008_ASADOMD10.msi

- Microsoft Server Speech Platform Runtime (x64)
  Platform\x64\SpeechPlatformRuntime.msi

- Microsoft Server Speech Recognition Language - TELE(en-US)
  SR\MSSpeech_SR_en-US_TELE.msi

- SQL 2008 R2 Reporting Services SharePoint 2010 Add-in
  1033\x64\rsSharePoint.msi

- Hotfix for WCF: SharePoint Shared Services Roll-up (Windows6.1-
  KB976462-v2-x64.msu)

Question	Besides installing the previous listed prerequisites, what other components does the prerequisite installer install and configure that are essential for SharePoint to function?
2	

Exercise 2.3	Install SharePoint 2010 Binaries
Overview	Now that the prerequisites are installed, in this exercise, you will install the SharePoint binaries.
Completion time	20 minutes

1. On your student server, log in as *contoso\Studentxx* (*xx* represents your student number) and use *Pa$$w0rd* as the password.

2. Click *Start* and in the *Search programs and files* search box, type *\\RWDC01\Downloads* and then press *Enter*.

3. Double-click the SharePoint executable (*sharepoint.exe*).

4. When the Microsoft Windows SharePoint 2010 splash screen displays, click the *Install SharePoint Server* option.

5. When prompted for the Product Key, type the key. The evaluation key for SharePoint Server 2010 with Enterprise Client Access License features is *VK7BD-VBKWR-6FHD9-Q3HM9-6PKMX*.

6. When the License Agreement displays, select the *I accept the terms of this License Agreement* check box and click *Continue*.

7. When prompted for the type of installation, click *Server Farm*.

8. Select the *Complete – Install all components* option.

9. Click *Install Now*.

10. When the Run Configuration Wizard box displays, make sure the *Run the SharePoint Products Configuration Wizard now* option is selected and then click *Close*.

11. When the SharePoint Configuration Wizard displays, click *Next*.

12. When you're warned that some services must be restarted, click *Yes*.

13. To create a new farm, select the *Create a new server farm* option and then click *Next*.

14. For the Database server, specify the name of the SQL server and its database name (*StudentXX*).

15. For the Username and Password, type *contoso\studentXX* and *Pa$$w0rd* and then click *Next*.

16. The passphrase is used to add servers to a farm. Type *Pa$$w0rd* for the passphrase in both text boxes and then click *Next*. The Configure SharePoint Central Administration Web Application page displays.

17. Select the *Specify port number* option and then type *3000* in the text box. Click *Next*.

18. When the Completing the SharePoint Products Configuration Wizard displays, click *Next*.

19. When the configuration is complete, click *Finish*. The SharePoint Central Administration tool displays.

20. When you are prompted to make SharePoint better, click *No, I don't wish to participate* and then click *OK*.

21. When you are prompted to choose how to configure your SharePoint farm, click *Start the Wizard*.

22. When prompted for a service account, type the *contoso\studentXX* account and then click *Next*.

23. After several minutes, you are asked to create the top-level Web site. In the Title text box, type the *StudentXX SharePoint*. Leave the Team Site template selected and click *OK*.

24. After the wizard completes, a summary screen displays.

25. Take a screen shot of the message box by pressing Alt+PrtScr and then use Ctrl+V to paste it into your Lab02_worksheet file in the page provided.

26. Click *Finish*.

27. Open Internet Explorer and go to *http://StudentXX* to verify that the SharePoint site is accessible.

28. Take a screen shot of the message box by pressing Alt+PrtScr and then use Ctrl+V to paste it into your Lab02_worksheet file in the page provided.

29. Close all windows.

30. Leave the computer logged on for the next exercise.

Exercise 2.4	Install SharePoint 2010 Service Pack 1
Overview	In this exercise, you will install SharePoint 2010 Service Pack 1.
Completion time	15 minutes

1. Click *Start* and in the *Search programs and files* search box, type *\\RWDC01\Downloads* and then press *Enter*.

2. Install SharePoint 2010 SP1 by double-clicking the *officeserver2010sp1-kb2460045-x64-fullfile-en-us.exe* file.

3. If you're prompted to make changes to the system, click *Yes*.

4. When the license agreement displays, click *Click here to accept the Microsoft Software License Terms* and then click *Continue*.

5. When you are prompted to reboot the computer, click *Yes*.

Exercise 2.5	Install the SharePoint 2010 Cumulative Patch
Overview	In the following exercise, you will install the SharePoint 2010 Cumulative patch.
Completion time	15 minutes

1. On your student server, log in as *contoso\Studentxx* (*xx* represents your student number) and use *Pa$$w0rd* as the password.

2. Click *Start* and in the *Search programs and files* search box, type *\\RWDC01\Downloads* and then press *Enter*.

3. To install the August 2011 cumulative update, double-click *office2010-kb2553048-fullfile-x64-glb.exe*.

4.   If a UAC warning displays, click *Yes*.

5.   When the license terms page displays, select *Click here to accept the Microsoft Software License Terms* and then click *Continue*.

6.   When the installation is complete, click *OK*.

Exercise 2.6	Run the SharePoint 2010 Products Configuration Tool
Overview	Any time you upgrade SharePoint, you should run the SharePoint 2010 Products Configuration Tool. Since you have just installed Service Pack 1 and a cumulative patch, in this lab you will run the SharePoint 2010 Products Configuration Tool.
Completion time	10 minutes

1.   Click *Start* > *All Programs* > *Microsoft SharePoint 2010 Products* > *SharePoint 2010 Products Configuration Wizard*.

2.   If a UAC dialog box displays, click *Yes*.

3.   When the Welcome to SharePoint Products page displays, click *Next*.

4.   When you are alerted that certain services must be restarted, click *Yes*.

5.   When the Completing the SharePoint Products Configuration Wizard opens, click *Next*.

6.   When the configuration is successful, take a screen shot of the message box by pressing Alt+PrtScr and then use Ctrl+V to paste it into your Lab02_worksheet file in the page provided.

7.   Click *Finish*. The Central Administration page displays.

8.   Open Internet Explorer and access *http://rwdc01* to verify the SharePoint site is accessible.

9.   Close Internet Explorer.

LAB 3
INSTALLING AND UPGRADING SHAREPOINT 2010 (PART II)

THIS LAB CONTAINS THE FOLLOWING EXERCISES AND ACTIVITIES:

Exercise 3.1	Look at the Installation Logs
Exercise 3.2	Install a Language Pack
Exercise 3.3	Copy and Upgrade a SharePoint 2010 Database
Exercise 3.4	Perform a Visual Upgrade
Lab Challenge	Create an Installation Script

BEFORE YOU BEGIN

The lab environment consists of student workstations connected to a local area network, along with a server that functions as the domain controller for a domain called contoso.com. The computers required for this lab are listed in Table 3-1.

Table 3-1
Computers required for Lab 3

Computer	Operating System	Computer Name
Instructor Server	Windows Server 2008 R2	RWDC01
Student Server	Windows Server 2008 R2	Student*xx*, *where xx* is your Student number.

> **NOTE**
>
> *In a classroom lab or virtual lab environment, there will be one classroom server and the students will have workstations named using consecutive numbers in place of the XX variable.*

In addition to the computers, you will also need the software listed in Table 3-2 in order to complete Lab 3.

Table 3-2
Software required for Lab 3

Software	Location
Windows Server 2008 R2 Multilingual User Interface Language Packs – French (Windows6.1-KB2483139-x64-fr-FR.exe)	\\rwdc01\downloads
2010 Server Language Packs for SharePoint Server 2010, Project Server 2010, Search Server 2010, and Office Web Apps 2010 – French (ServerLanguagePack.exe)	\\rwdc01\downloads
SharePoint Installation Files	\\rwdc01\downloads\SharePoint2010
WSS_Content_30.bak	\\rwdc01\downloads
Lab 3 student worksheet	Lab03_worksheet.rtf (provided by instructor)

Working with Lab Worksheets

Each lab in this manual requires that you answer questions, shoot screen shots, and perform other activities that you will document in a worksheet named for the lab (such as Lab03_worksheet.rtf). Your instructor will provide you with access to the worksheets. It is recommended that you use a USB flash drive to store your worksheets, so you can submit them to your instructor for review. As you perform the exercises in each lab, open the appropriate worksheet file using WordPad, fill in the required information, and save the file to your flash drive.

SCENARIO

You have just completed the installation and patching of SharePoint 2010. Now you need to verify if the installation had any errors. You then need to prepare the SharePoint site to support additional languages. Lastly, you must migrate the content database from your previous version of SharePoint and upgrade the database so that it can be accessed from the users.

After completing this lab, you will be able to:

- Analyze the SharePoint 2010 installation logs

- Install a language pack

- Upgrade a WSS 3.0 content database

- Perform a visual upgrade of a SharePoint 2010 site

Estimated lab time: 60 minutes

Exercise 3.1	Look at the Installation Logs
Overview	In the following exercise, you will look at the application logs in the event viewer and the installation logs for SharePoint.
Completion time	10 minutes

1. On your student server, log in as *contoso\Studentxx* (*xx* represents your student number) and use *Pa$$w0rd* as the password.

2. Click *Start*, right-click *Computer*, and then select *Manage*. Server Manager displays.

3. Expand *Diagnostics*, expand *Event Viewer*, expand *Windows Logs*, and then click *Application*.

4. Quickly browse the events since and during the installation, looking for errors and warnings.

5. In the *Actions* pane, click the *Filter Current Log*.

6. Select *Critical*, *Warning* and *Error* and then click *OK*.

7. Again, review the errors that have appeared since and during your installation of SharePoint.

8. In the *Windows Log* section in the left pane, click *System*.

9. Review the errors and warnings that have appeared since and during your installation of SharePoint.

10. Close *Server Manager*.

11. Using Windows Explorer, navigate to the *C:\Program Files\Common Files\Microsoft Shared\Web Server Extensions\14\LOGS* folder.

12. Right-click the most recent PSCDiagnostics file and then select *Open with*.

Question 1	What are the PSCDiagnostic logs used for?

13. Click the plus sign (+) next to *Other Programs*. Double-click *Notepad*.

14. Quickly browse through the log file.

15. Go back to the beginning of the log file.

16. Open Notepad's *Edit* menu and select *Find*. In the *Find what* text box, type *error* and then click *Find Next*.

17. Review the line that displays the error.

18. Press *Find Next* to view all lines that include this error.

19. When you have searched the document, close the *Find* dialog box and close *Notepad*.

20. The Student*XX-<date>-<time>*.log files are the log files for SharePoint. Right-click the oldest log file and select *Open with*.

21. Click the plus sign (+) next to *Other Programs*. Double-click *Notepad*.

22. Similar to the PSCDiagnostics file, search for and review the lines with errors.

23. Close *Notepad*.

Question 2	What logs are for the SharePoint 2010 Products Configuration Wizard?

24. Open the *Upgrade-<date>-<time>.log* file using Notepad.

Question 3	Are there any other logs files in the LOGS folder? What are these logs files used for?

25. Close *Notepad*.

Exercise 3.2	Install a Language Pack
Overview	In the following exercise, you will install a Windows and SharePoint language pack and then create a site based on the language installed.
Completion time	20 minutes

1. Click *Start*, and in the *Search Programs and Files* search box, type *\\RWDC01\Downloads* and then press *Enter*.

2. Double-click *Windows6.1-KB2483139-x64-fr-FR.exe*. The Install or uninstall display languages dialog box displays while the French language pack is being installed.

3. After the Windows display pack is installed, double-click the *ServerLanguagePack.exe* file.

4. Click the *J'accepte les termes de ce contrat* option and then click *Continuer*.

5. Leave the *Executer l'Assistant Configuration des produits SharePoint* option selected and then click *Fermer*.

6. When the *Welcome to SharePoint Products* option displays, click *Next*.

7. When you are prompted to restart some services, click *Yes*.

8. When the configuration is successful, click *Finish*.

9. Click *Start > All Programs > Microsoft SharePoint 2010 Products > SharePoint 2010 Central Administration*.

10. Click *Application Management*.

11. Click *Create Site collections*.

12. In the *Title* text box, type *French Site*.

13. In the *URL* text box, specify the *http://Studentxx/sites/French*

14. For the *Language* option, select *French*.

15. Click *OK*.

16. Click *http://Studentxx/sites/French*.

17. Close Internet Explorer.

Exercise 3.3	Copy and Upgrade a SharePoint Database
Overview	During this exercise, you will copy a content database from WSS 3.0 to your SharePoint 2010 installation and then upgrade the database.
Completion time	25 minutes

1. Click *Start*, and in the *Search Programs and Files* search box, type *\\RWDC01\Downloads* and then press *Enter*.

2. Copy the *WSS_Content_30.bak* file to the *C:\Program Files\Microsoft SQL Server\MSSQL10_50.MSSQLSERVER\MSSQL\Backup* folder.

3. Click *Start > All Programs > Microsoft SQL Server 2008 R2 > SQL Server Management Studio*.

4. When you are prompted to connect to a server, make sure the server type is set to *Database Engine* and the server name is set to *StudentXX*. Click *Connect*.

5. Right-click *Databases* and select *Restore Database*.

6. When the Restore Database dialog box displays, click the *From device* option and click the . . . button.

7. When the Specify Backup dialog box displays, click *Add*.

8. In the *C:\Program Files\Microsoft SQL Server\MSSQL10_50.MSSQLSERVER\MSSQL\Backup* folder, double-click *WSS_Content_30.bak*.

9. In the Specify Backup dialog box, click *OK*.

10. In the Restore Database dialog box, for the *To database* option, select *WSS_Content_30*. Select the check box in the *Restore* column. Click *OK*.

11. When the restore is complete, click *OK*.

12. In Microsoft SQL Server Management Studio, expand *Databases* and then verify that *WSS_Content_30* is there.

13. Close *Microsoft SQL Server Management Studio*.

14. Click *Start > All Programs > Microsoft SharePoint 2010 Products > SharePoint 2010 Central Administration*.

15. Click *Application Management*.

16. Click *Manage Web applications*.

17. On the Ribbon, click **New**. The Create New Web Application page displays.

18. Change the port to *8080*.

19. Click inside the *Path* text box to see the IIS Web site name to change.

20. Click *OK* to create the new Web Application.

21. When the application is created, click *OK*.

22. You should see the newly created application.

23. Click *Start > All Programs > Microsoft SharePoint 2010 Products > SharePoint 2010 Management Shell*.

24. Execute the following command in the Management Shell (whereby *XX* is your student number):

    ```
    test-spcontentdatabase -name wss_content_30 -
    webapplication http://studentXX:8080
    ```

25. Look for any issues that might cause the upgrade to fail.

26. To mount the database, execute the following command:

    ```
    Mount-spcontentdatabase -name wss_content_30 -
    databaseserver studentXX -webapplication
    http://studentXX:8080
    ```

27. Open Internet Explorer and go to *http://studentXX:8080*.

28. Open *Central Administration*.

29. In the *Upgrade and Migration* section, click *Check upgrade status*.

30. Verify that the status succeeded and that there are no errors.

31. Close *Central Administration*.

Exercise 3.4	Perform a Visual Upgrade
Overview	In the following exercise, you will upgrade the WSS 3.0 interface of an upgraded database to a SharePoint 2010 interface.
Completion time	5 minutes

1. Open Internet Explorer and go to *http://studentXX:8080*.

2. Click the *WSS 3.0 Subsite*.

3.   Open the *Site Actions* menu and select *Visual Upgrade*.

4.   Select the *Preview the updated user interface* and click *OK*.

5.   On the yellow bar at the top of the screen, click *View or modify this site's Visual upgrade settings*.

6.   Click *Update the user interface* and click *OK*.

LAB CHALLENGE: CREATE AN INSTALLATION SCRIPT

Completion time   15 minutes

Create a batch file that installs all of the prerequisites from the \\rwdc01\downloads and then installs the SharePoint binaries. You also must create the Config.XML file used for the unattended installation. If you need assistance, execute one of the following commands from the installation files (\\rwdc01\downloads\Sharepoint2010):

```
Prerequisiteinstaller.exe /?

Setup.exe /?
```

In addition, you can access the sample xml files from \\rwdc01\Downloads\SharePoint2010\Files.

LAB 4
CONFIGURING
SHAREPOINT 2010

THIS LAB CONTAINS THE FOLLOWING EXERCISES AND ACTIVITIES:

THIS LAB CONTAINS THE FOLLOWING EXERCISES AND ACTIVITIES:

Exercise 4.1	Configure SharePoint 2010
Exercise 4.2	Configure Email
Exercise 4.3	Use stsadm Commands
Exercise 4.4	Use PowerShell Commands

BEFORE YOU BEGIN

The lab environment consists of student workstations connected to a local area network, along with a server that functions as the domain controller for a domain called contoso.com. The computers required for this lab are listed in Table 4-1.

Table 4-1
Computers required for Lab 4

Computer	Operating System	Computer Name
Instructor Server	Windows Server 2008 R2	RWDC01
Student Server	Windows Server 2008 R2	Studentxx, where xx is your Student number.

> **NOTE**
> *In a classroom lab or virtual lab environment, there will be one classroom server and the students will have workstations named using consecutive numbers in place of the XX variable.*

In addition to the computers, you will also need the software listed in Table 4-2 in order to complete Lab 4.

Table 4-2
Software required for Lab 4

Software	Location
Lab 4 student worksheet	Lab04_worksheet.rtf (provided by instructor)

Working with Lab Worksheets

Each lab in this manual requires that you answer questions, shoot screen shots, and perform other activities that you will document in a worksheet named for the lab (such as Lab04_worksheet.rtf). Your instructor will provide you with access to the worksheets. It is recommended that you use a USB flash drive to store your worksheets, so you can submit them to your instructor for review. As you perform the exercises in each lab, open the appropriate worksheet file using WordPad, fill in the required information, and save the file to your flash drive.

SCENARIO

Now that SharePoint has been installed, you are now ready to configure basic functionality. In this lab, you will use SharePoint Central Administrator to review the current configuration and make sure the basic services are enabled and configured.

After completing this lab, you will be able to:

- Configure SharePoint 2010 with Central Administration

- Use `Stsadm` to manage SharePoint 2010

- Use SharePoint PowerShell to manage SharePoint 2010

Estimated lab time: 55 minutes

Exercise 4.1	Configure SharePoint 2010
Overview	In the following exercise, you will use Central Administration to configure SharePoint and to review its current configuration.
Completion time	20 minutes

1. On your student server, login as contoso\student*xx* (*xx* represents your student number) with the password of *Pa$$w0rd*.

2. Click *Start* > *All Programs* > *Microsoft SharePoint 2010 Products* > *SharePoint 2010 Central Administration*. Central Administration displays.

3. Click *System Settings*.

4. Click *Manage servers in this farm*. The Servers in Farm page displays.

Question 1	What is the configuration database version?

Question 2	Where is the configuration database located and what is the name of the configuration database?

5. In the Server column, click *StudentXX*. The Services on Server page displays.

Question 3	Which services are stopped?

6. To stop the Microsoft SharePoint Foundation Workflow Timer Service, click *Stop* in the row with Microsoft SharePoint Foundation Workflow Timer Service. If you are prompted to continue, click *OK*.

7. To start the Microsoft SharePoint Foundation Workflow Timer Service, click *Start* in the row with Microsoft SharePoint Foundation Workflow Timer Service.

8. The services that can be configured are blue. Click *Microsoft SharePoint Foundation Workflow Timer Service*.

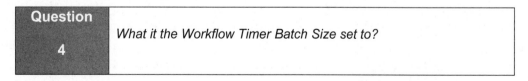

Question 4	What it the Workflow Timer Batch Size set to?

9. Click *Cancel*.

10. At the top of the page, click *Central Administration*.

11. Click *Upgrade and Migration*.

12. Click *Enable Enterprise Features*. The Enable Enterprise Features page displays.

13. Click *Cancel*.

14. Click the *Enable Features on Existing Sites*. The Enable Features on existing sites page displays.

15. Select the *Enable all sites in this installation to use the following set of features* and click *OK*.

16. Click *Close*.

17. Click *Check product and patch installation status*.

18. In Internet Explorer, click the *Back arrow*.

19. Click *Review database status*.

20. Make sure that all databases do not need action to be done.

21. Click the *wss_content_30* database.

22. To prevent the creation of new site collections, change the database status from Ready to *Offline*.

23. Click *OK*.

24. Click the *wss_content_30* database.

25. To remove the content database, select the *Remove content database* option. If you're prompted to remove the database, click *OK*.

26. Click *OK* again.

27. On the left side of the page, click *Application Management*. The Application Management page displays.

28. In the Databases section, click *Manage content databases*.

Question 5	What is the name of the current content database used on SharePoint?

29. On the left side of the page, click *General Application Settings*.

30. In the SharePoint Designer section, click *Configure SharePoint Designer settings*. The SharePoint Designer Settings page displays.

Question 6	*Is the use of SharePoint Designer with SharePoint 2010 enabled by default?*

31. Click *OK*.

32. On the left side of the page, click *Security*. The Security page displays.

33. Click the *Manage the farm administrators* group.

Question 7	*Who are the default farm administrators?*

34. In Internet Explorer, click the *Back arrow*.

35. Click the *Defined blocked file types* option.

36. To block all files that have a filename extension gts, type *gts* at the end of the list on its own line.

37. Click *OK*.

38. Click the *Managed antivirus settings* option.

Question 8	*Is Antivirus Settings enabled by default?*

39. Click *Cancel*.

40. Close Internet Explorer.

Exercise 4.2	Configure Email
Overview	In the following exercise, you will configure outgoing and incoming e-mail settings.
Completion time	15 minutes

1. Click *Start* > *All Programs* > *Microsoft SharePoint 2010 Products* > *SharePoint 2010 Central Administration*. Central Administration displays.

2. Click *System Settings*.

3. Click *Configure outgoing e-mail settings*.

4. For the *Outbound SMTP server* setting, type *rwdc01.contoso.com*.

5. For the *From address* and the *Reply-to address* settings, type *SharePointXX@paccoast.com*.

6. Click *OK*.

7. Click *Start*, right-click *Computer*, and then select *Manage*.

8. Click *Features* and then click *Add Features*. The Select Features dialog box displays.

9. Select *SMTP Server* and then click *Install*. When you're prompted to add additional roles for SMTP, click *Add Required Role Services*. Click *Next*.

10. When the Web Server (IIS) introduction page displays, click *Next*.

11. When the Select Role Services page displays, click *Next*.

12. When the Confirm Installation Selections page displays, click *Install*.

13. When the Installation Results page displays, click *Close*.

14. Close Server Manager.

15. Go back to the *System Settings* page of Central Administration.

16. Click *Configure incoming e-mail settings*.

17. Select *Enable sites on this server to receive e-mail*.

Question 9	What is the incoming E-Mail Server Display Address?

18. Click *OK*.

19. Use Internet Explorer to open *http://studentXX*.

20. Under Lists, click *Calendar*.

21.   On the Ribbon, in the *Calendar Tools* section, click *Calendar*

22.   On the Ribbon, click *List Settings*.

23.   In the Communications section, click *Incoming e-mail settings*.

24.   To allow this list to receive e-mail, click *Yes*.

25.   For the address, specify *Calendar@studentXX.contoso.com*.

26.   Click *OK*.

27.   Close Internet Explorer.

Exercise 4.3	Use stsadm Commands
Overview	In the following exercise, you will learn how to use stsadm commands.
Completion time	10 minutes

1.   Click *Start* > *All Programs* > *Accessories*. Right-click *Command Prompt* and select *Run as administrator*.

2.   At the command prompt, change to the *C:\Program Files\Common files\Microsoft Shared\Web Server Extensions\14\Bin* folder.

3.   To view the help for stsadm, execute the following command:

```
stsadm -help
```

4.   To see the Admin port used by SharePoint Central Admin, execute the following command:

```
stsadm -o getadminport
```

Question 10	*What is the current admin port?*

5.   To create a site, execute the following command (*XX* is your student number):

```
stsadm -o createsite -url
http://studentXX/sites/stsadmsite -owneremail
studentXX@contoso.com -ownerlogin contoso\studentXX
```

6.   Open Internet Explorer and go to *http://studentXX/sites/stsadmsite*.

7. Select the *Team Site* template and click *OK*. When you are prompted for the groups for the site, click *OK*.

8. To delete the stsadmsite site that you just created, execute the following command at the command prompt:

    ```
    stsadm -o deletesite -url
    http://studentXX/sites/stsadmsite
    ```

9. Close the command prompt window.

Exercise 4.4	Use PowerShell Commands
Overview	In the following exercise, you will learn how to use the PowerShell commands to manage SharePoint 2010.
Completion time	10 minutes

1. Click *Start* > *All Programs* > *Microsoft SharePoint 2010 Products.* Right-click *SharePoint 2010 Management Shell* and select *Run as Administrator*.

2. To create an *http://studentXX//sites/powershelllsite* site, execute the following commands with PowerShell (whereby *XX* is your student number).

    ```
    $template = Get-SPWebTemplate "STS#0"

    New-SPSite -Url
    "http://studentXX/sites/powershellsite" -OwnerAlias
    "corporate\StudentXX" -Template $template
    ```

3. Open Internet Explorer and go to *http://studentXX/sites/powershellsite*.

4. Close Internet Explorer.

5. To view your sites, execute the following PowerShell command (*XX* is your student number):

    ```
    get-spweb -identity http://StudentXX
    ```

6. To change the admin port for SharePoint Central Administration to 4000, execute the following command:

    ```
    Set-SPCentralAdministration -Port 4000
    ```

7. When you're prompted to confirm this action, type *y* and then press *Enter*.

8. Open *Central Administration* and verify that it now uses port 4000.

9. Close *Central Administration*.

10. Close PowerShell.

LAB 5
DEPLOYING AND MANAGING WEB APPLICATIONS AND SITE COLLECTIONS

THIS LAB CONTAINS THE FOLLOWING EXERCISES AND ACTIVITIES:

Exercise 5.1 Create and Delete Web Applications

Exercise 5.2 Configure SSL for SharePoint

Exercise 5.3 Modify Access Mappings

Exercise 5.4 Extend a Web Application

Exercise 5.5 Manage Web Application Settings

Exercise 5.6 Use Managed Paths

Exercise 5.7 Manage Site Collections

BEFORE YOU BEGIN

The lab environment consists of student workstations connected to a local area network, along with a server that functions as the domain controller for a domain called contoso.com. The computers required for this lab are listed in Table 5-1.

Table 5-1
Computers required for Lab 5

Computer	Operating System	Computer Name
Instructor Server	Windows Server 2008 R2	RWDC01
Student Server	Windows Server 2008 R2	Student*xx, where xx* is your Student number.

> **NOTE**
>
> *In a classroom lab or virtual lab environment, there will be one classroom server and the students will have workstations named using consecutive numbers in place of the XX variable.*

In addition to the computers, you will also need the software listed in Table 5-2 in order to complete Lab 5.

Table 5-2
Software required for Lab 5

Software	Location
Lab 5 student worksheet	Lab05_worksheet.rtf (provided by instructor)

Working with Lab Worksheets

Each lab in this manual requires that you answer questions, shoot screen shots, and perform other activities that you will document in a worksheet named for the lab (such as Lab05_worksheet.rtf). Your instructor will provide you with access to the worksheets. It is recommended that you use a USB flash drive to store your worksheets, so you can submit them to your instructor for review. As you perform the exercises in each lab, open the appropriate worksheet file using WordPad, fill in the required information, and save the file to your flash drive.

SCENARIO

Now that you have taken care of SharePoint's basic configuration, you need to configure SharePoint so that it can be used by users, including creating Web applications and creating site collections.

After completing this lab, you will be able to:

- Create and manage Web applications

- Configure a Web application to support SSL

- Manage managed paths

- Create, delete, and manage site collections

Estimated lab time: 90 minutes

Exercise 5.1	Create and Delete Web Applications
Overview	In the following exercise, you will create and delete Web applications.
Completion time	15 minutes

1. On your student server, log in as *contoso\Studentxx* (*xx* represents your student number) and use *Pa$$w0rd* as the password.

2. Click *Start* > *All Programs* > *Microsoft SharePoint 2010 Products* > *SharePoint 2010 Central Administration*. Central Administration displays.

3. In the Application Management section, click *Manage Web applications*.

4. On the Ribbon, click *New*.

5. On the Create New Web Application page, in the *Authentication* section, click *Classic Mode Authentication*.

6. In the *IIS Web Site* section, in the *Port* text box, type *81*.

Question	
1	*What is the path for the IIS Web site?*

7. In the *Database Name and Authentication* section, change the database name to *wss_content_81*.

8. Click *OK* to create the new Web application.

9. When the application is created, click *OK*.

10. Launch Internet Explorer and go to *http://studentxx:81*.

Question	
2	*What error message did you get? Why did you get this error?*

11. Go back to the *Central Administration Web Applications Management* page.

12. On the left side of the page, click *Application Management*.

13. Click *Create site collections*.

14. On the Web Application page, change the Web application to *http://StudentXX:81*.

15. In the *Title* text box, type *Test SharePoint*.

16. In the *Username* text box, type *StudentXX* (*XX* is your student number).

17. Click *OK*.

18. When the Top-Level Site is successfully created, click *OK*.

19. Launch Internet Explorer and go to *http://studentxx:81*.

20. Go back to *Central Administration*.

21. Click *Application Management* and then click *Manage Web applications*.

22. Click the *SharePoint – 81* Web application to select it.

23. Click *Delete*. The Delete Web Application page displays.

24. Select *Yes* to delete the content databases and click *Yes* to delete IIS Web sites. Click *Delete*.

25. When you are prompted to confirm this action, click *OK*.

Exercise 5.2	Configure SSL for SharePoint
Overview	In the following exercise, you will create a Web application that is configured to use SSL. You will then create a self-signed digital certificate and apply it to the related IIS Web site.
Completion time	20 minutes

1. Open *Central Administration*.

2. In the *Application Management* section, click Manage *Web Applications*.

3. On the Ribbon, click *New*.

4. Change the port to *6000*.

5. Select *Yes* to use Secure Sockets Layer (SSL).

6. Change the public URL to *https://studentXX.contoso.com:6000* (*XX* is your student number).

7. Change the database name to *WSS_Content_SSL*.

8. Click *OK*.

9. When the application is created, click *OK*.

10. Click *Application Management* and then, in the *Site Collections* section, click *Create site collections*.

11. In the *Title* text box, type *SSL*.

12. In the *URL* text box, type *SSL*

13. In the primary *Site Collection Administration* text box, type *StudentXX* (*XX* is your student number).

14. Click *OK* to create the site collection.

15. When the site collection is created, click *OK*.

16. Click *Start* > *Administrative Tools* > *Internet Information Services (IIS) Manager*.

17. In the left pane, click the name of the server (*StudentXX*).

18. In the center pane, in the *IIS* section, click *Server Certificates*.

19. In the *Actions* section, click *Open Features*.

20. In the *Actions* section, click *Create Self-signed Certificate*.

21. In the *Friendly Name* text box, type **.contoso.com* and then click *OK*.

22. In the left pane of IIS Manager, expand *Sites*.

23. Right-click the *SharePoint – 6000* site and then select *Edit Bindings*.

24. Click the current binding for port *6000* and then click *Edit*.

25. For the SSL certificate, choose **.contoso.com*.

26. To see the certificate, click *View*.

Question	
3	*When does the certificate expire?*

27. Click *OK* to accept your settings and close the Certificate dialog box.

28. Click *OK* to accept your settings and close the Edit Site Binding dialog box.

29. Click *Close* to close the Site Bindings dialog box.

30. Right-click *SharePoint – 6000*, click *Manage Web Site*, and then click *Restart*.

31. Launch Internet Explorer and go to ***https://StudentXX.contoso.com:6000***. If you see a certificate error, you would normally be concerned. Because this is a self-signed certificate, usually used for testing, you know that the error can be safely ignored. However, if you were going into production and you were to put this site on the Internet, you would have to purchase a third-party digital certificate.

Exercise 5.3	Modify Access Mappings
Overview	In the following exercise, you will add an internal URL to a Web application and modify the IIS site to respond to the site.
Completion time	10 minutes

1. Open *Central Administration* and click *Application Management*.

2. In the *Web Applications* section, click *Configure alternate access mappings*.

3. Click *Alternate Access Mapping Collection* and then select *Change Alternate Access Mapping Collection*.

4. Click *SharePoint – 80*.

5. Click *Add Internal URLs*. The Add Internal URLs page displays.

6. In the *URL* text box, type ***http://intranet*** and then select the *Intranet zone*. Click *Save*.

7. Click *Start > Administrative Tools > Internet Information Services (IIS) Manager*.

8. In the left pane, expand *Sites*.

9. Right-click *SharePoint – 80* site and select *Edit Bindings*.

10. Click *Add*.

11. In the *Host name* text box, type *intranet*.

12. Click *OK* to accept your settings and close the Edit Site Bindings dialog box.

13. Click *Close* to close the Site Bindings dialog box.

14. Because your current DNS system does not provide name resolution for an intranet, you must modify the host file to provide name resolution. To start with that, you must determine the IP address of the system. Therefore, click *Start > All Programs > Accessories > Command Prompt*. The Command Prompt displays.

15. To determine the IP address, execute the following command:

```
ipconfig
```

Question 4	What is the IPv4 address of your system?

16. Click **Start** > **Computer**.

17. Using Windows Explorer, navigate to the **C:\Windows\System32\drivers\etc** folder.

18. Double-click the **hosts** file. When the **Open with** window displays, double-click **Notepad**. The hosts file opens in Notepad.

19. At the end of the host file (on its own line), type the following line:

    <Your IP address>   intranet

    For example, **10.10.0.101   intranet**

20. Save the file in Notepad and then close Notepad.

21. Launch Internet Explorer and go to the **http://intranet** Web site.

22. Close Internet Explorer.

Exercise 5.4	Extend a Web Application
Overview	In the following exercise, you will extend a Web application to respond to a second name.
Completion time	10 minutes

1. Open **Central Administration** and click **Manage Web applications**.

2. Click to select the **SharePoint – 80** Web site.

3. On the Ribbon, click **Extend**.

4. Change the port to **5000**.

5. In the **Host Header** text box, type **partner.contoso.com**.

6. In the **Public URL** section, for the **Zone** setting, select **Extranet**.

7. Click **OK** to extend the Web site.

8. To provide name resolution for Extranet, you must add a line in the host file for Extranet. Click *Start* > *Computer*.

9. Using Windows Explorer, navigate to the *C:\Windows\System32\drivers\etc* folder.

10. Double-click the *hosts* file. When the *Open with* window displays, double-click *Notepad*. The hosts file opens in Notepad.

11. At the end of the host file (on its own line), type the following line:

    <Your IP address>   partner.contoso.com

    For example, **10.10.0.101**   **partner.contoso.com**

12. Save the file in Notepad and then close Notepad.

13. Open Internet Explorer and go to the *http://partner.contoso.com* Web site. When you're prompted to log in, log in with *contoso\StudentXX* (*XX* is the student number).

14. As a security feature built into Windows server, by default, the server responds only to a request sent to it by the name of the server. It does not respond to other names, although the IP address points to the server. Therefore, you must disable loopback checking. To disable loopback, click *Start* and, in the *Search programs and files* search box, type *regedit* and then press *Enter*.

15. Navigate to the following key:

    HKEY_LOCAL_Machine\System\CurrentControlSet\Control\LSA.

16. If the DisableLoopBackCheck does not exist, right-click *LSA*, click *New*, and then click *DWORD (32-bit) Value*. In the *Name* text box, type *DisableLoopbackCheck* and then press *Enter*.

17. Double-click the *DisableLoopbackCheck* value and, in the *Value data* text box, type *1*.

18. Click *OK* to accept your settings and close Edit DWORD (32-bit) Value.

19. Close Registry Editor.

20. Launch Internet Explorer and go to *http://partner.contoso.com*.

Exercise 5.5	Manage Web Application Settings
Overview	In the following exercise, you will modify settings assigned to a Web application, including configuring the browser file handling, the Recycle Bin, and the list threshold.
Completion time	10 minutes

1.   Open *Central Administration*.

2.   In the *Application Management* section, click *Manage Web Applications*.

3.   Click the *SharePoint – 6000* Web application.

4.   On the Ribbon, click *General Settings*.

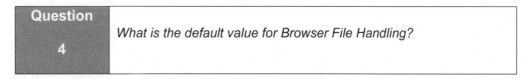

Question 4	What is the default value for Browser File Handling?

5.   Scroll down to *Recycle Bin*.

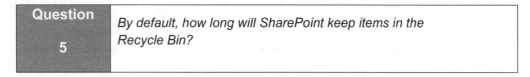

Question 5	By default, how long will SharePoint keep items in the Recycle Bin?

6.   Change the maximum upload size to *100* MB.

7.   Click *OK*.

8.   Click the *SharePoint – 6000* Web application.

9.   Click the small down arrow on the *General Settings* button and then select *Resource Throttling*.

Question 6	What is the default List View Threshold?

Question 7	What is the List View Threshold for Auditors and Administrators?

10. Change the List View Threshold to *6000*.

11. Click *OK* to accept your settings and close the Resource Throttling page.

12. Click the *SharePoint – 6000* Web application.

13. To disable user-defined workflows, click the *General Settings* down arrow and then select *Workflow*. The Workflow Settings dialog box displays.

14. Select *No* for the *Enable user-defined workflows for all sites on this Web application* option.

15. Click **OK** to accept your settings and close the Workflow Settings page.

16. Click the **SharePoint – 6000** Web application.

17. On the Ribbon, click the **Web Application Blocked File Types** button.

18. To allow ksh files for this Web application, find the line of **ksh** and delete the line.

19. Click **OK** to close the Blocked File Types.

20. Leave the Web applications page open for the next execise.

Exercise 5.6	Use Managed Paths
Overview	In the following exercise, you will add a new managed path and create a site collection under the managed path.
Completion time	10 minutes

1. Click the **SharePoint – 6000** Web application to highlight it and then click **Managed Paths**.

2. In the **Path** text box, type **Projects**.

3. Click **Add Path**.

4. Click **OK** to accept your settings and close the Defined Managed Paths dialog.

5. Launch Internet Explorer and go to **https://StudentXX.contoso.com:6000**.

6. Click the **Site Actions** menu and select **New Site**.

7. On the left side of the page, click **Application Management**.

8. Click **Create site collections**.

9. In the **Title** text box, type **Project #1**.

10. In the **Web site address** text box, type **https://StudentXX:6000:/projects/project1**.

11. Select the **Team Site** template.

12. Specify the **Primary Site Collection Administrator** as **StudentXX** (*XX* is your student number).

13. Click **OK**.

14. When the Top-Level Site is successfully created, click **https://StudentXX:6000/projects/project1**.

15. Close the Project1 site.

16. Close **Central Administration**.

Exercise 5.7	Managing Site Collections
Overview	In the following exercise, you will modify settings related to a site collection, including adding site collection administrators, enabling caches for site collections, enabling auditing, and recreating a retention policy.
Completion time	15 minutes

1. Launch **Internet Explorer** and go to **http://StudentXX**.

2. Click the **Site Actions** menu and then click **Site Settings**.

3. In the **Users and Permissions** section, click **Site collection administrators**.

4. In the **Site Collection Administrators** section, add the **domain admins** group. Click **OK**.

5. In the **Site Collection Administration** section, click **Site collection object cache**.

6. Increase the maximum cache size to **200** MB.

7. Click **OK**.

8. In the **Site Collection Administration** section, click **Site collection output cache**.

9. Click **Enable output cache**.

10. In the **Authenticated Cache Profile** section, select **Intranet (Collaboration Site)**.

11. Click **OK**.

12. On the Site Settings page, click **Site Collection audit settings**.

13. Select **Yes** to automatically trim the audit log.

14. Specify **90** days to keep retain the audit log data.

15. In the **Documents and Items** section, select **Editing items** and **Deleting or restoring items**.

16. In the **Lists, Libraries, and Sites** section, click **Editing content types and columns** and **Editing users and permissions**.

17. Click **OK** to save the audit settings.

18. Using Internet Explorer, go to **http://studentXX**.

19. Click **Shared Documents**.

20. Open *WordPad*. Type your name into the document and then save the document to your desktop with the file name *student.rtf*.

21. Click *Add document*.

22. Click *Browse*. Navigate to the desktop, double-click *Student.rtf*, and then click *Open*.

23. Click *OK* to close the Upload Document page.

24. Delete the Student document from the Shared Documents by checking the box next to the document and clicking *Delete*. When you are prompted to confirm, click *OK*.

25. Go back to *http://StudentXX*.

26. Click *Site Actions* and click *Site Settings*.

27. In the *Site Collection Administration* section, click *Audit log reports*.

28. In the *Content Activity Reports* section, click *Deletion*.

29. Click *Browse*, select *Documents*, and then click *OK*.

30. On the *Customize* page, click *OK*.

31. Click the *Click here to view the report* link.

32. When the File Download dialog box displays, click *Open*. Microsoft Excel opens.

33. Click the *Report Data 1* tab.

34. Close Microsoft Excel.

35. On the Operation Completed Successfully page, click *OK*.

36. Back on the Site settings page, in the *Site Collection Administration* section, click *Site collection policies*. The Policies page displays.

37. Click the *Create* link.

38. In the *Name* text box, type *Policy*.

39. Click to select *Retention*.

40. Click the *Add a retention stage . . .* link.

41. With the *This stage is based off a date property on the item* selected, specify *2 years* and then click *OK*.

42. Click *OK* to save the policy.

43. Close Internet Explorer.

LAB 6
DEPLOYING AND MANAGING SHAREPOINT 2010 FEATURES AND SOLUTIONS

BEFORE YOU BEGIN

The lab environment consists of student workstations connected to a local area network, along with a server that functions as the domain controller for a domain called contoso.com. The computers required for this lab are listed in Table 6-1.

Table 6-1
Computers required for Lab 6

Computer	Operating System	Computer Name
Instructor Server	Windows Server 2008 R2	RWDC01
Student Server	Windows Server 2008 R2	Student*xx*, *where xx* is your Student number.

> **NOTE**
>
> *In a classroom lab or virtual lab environment, there will be one classroom server and the students will have workstations named using consecutive numbers in place of the XX variable.*

In addition to the computers, you will also need the software listed in Table 6-2 in order to complete Lab 6.

Table 6-2
Software required for Lab 6

Software	Location
SharePointLogger.wsp and PrintList.wsp	\\rwdc01\downloads
Lab 6 student worksheet	Lab06_worksheet.rtf (provided by instructor)

Working with Lab Worksheets

Each lab in this manual requires that you answer questions, shoot screen shots, and perform other activities that you will document in a worksheet named for the lab (such as Lab06_worksheet.rtf). Your instructor will provide you with access to the worksheets. It is recommended that you use a USB flash drive to store your worksheets, so you can submit them to your instructor for review. As you perform the exercises in each lab, open the appropriate worksheet file using WordPad, fill in the required information, and save the file to your flash drive.

SCENARIO

Now that you have created your SharePoint environment has been created, you need to work closely with your development team to install the solutions created by the development team. In addition, you also need to make it possible for the development team to test new, untested solutions that will not take down the entire SharePoint environment if something goes wrong.

After completing this lab, you will be able to:

■ Install and uninstall farm solutions

■ Enable the SharePoint sandbox

■ Deploy solutions to the SharePoint sandbox

■ Enable the Developer Dashboard

Estimated lab time: 45 minutes

Exercise 6.1	Install and Uninstall Solutions
Overview	In the following exercise, you will install and uninstall a solution in SharePoint.
Completion time	10 minutes

1. On your student server, log in as *contoso\Studentxx* (*xx* represents your student number) and use *Pa$$w0rd* as the password.

2. Click *Start > All Programs > Microsoft SharePoint 2010 Products > SharePoint 2010 Management Shell*.

3. To add the sharepointlogger.wsp solution, execute the following command at the PowerShell prompt:

```
Add-spsolution -literalpath
\\rwdc01\downloads\sharepointlogger.wsp
```

4. Open *Central Administration*.

5. On the Central Administration page, click *System Settings*.

6. In the Farm Management section, click *Manage farm solutions*. The Solution Management page displays.

7. Click the *sharepointlogger.wsp* solution that you want to deploy. The Solution Properties page displays.

8. Click *Deploy Solution*. The Deploy Solution page displays.

9. On the Deploy Solution page, in the *Deploy When?* section, click *Now* and then click *OK*.

10. To retract the solution, click *sharepointlogger.wsp* on the Solution Management page.

11. On the Solution Properties page, click ***Retract Solution***.

12. With the Retract configured to *Now*, click ***OK***.

13. Go back to the PowerShell prompt.

14. To remove the solution, execute the following command:

    ```
    Remove-SPSolution -Identity sharepointlogger.wsp
    ```

15. When you are prompted to confirm this action, press the *a* key on the keyboard.

16. Close the PowerShell window and close Internet Explorer.

Exercise 6.2	Install a SharePoint Sandbox
Overview	In the following exercise, you will install the SharePoint sandbox so that you can install sandbox solutions.
Completion time	5 minutes

1. Open ***Central Administration***.

2. In the ***System Settings*** section, click ***Manage services on server***. The Services on Server page displays.

3. In the ***Action*** column for the ***Microsoft SharePoint Foundation Sandboxed Code Service,*** click ***Start***.

4. Click ***System Settings***. The System Settings page displays.

5. In the ***Farm Management*** section, click ***Manage user solutions***. The Sandboxed Solution Management page displays.

6. In the ***Load Balancing*** section, select ***All sandboxed code runs on the same machine as a request.***

7. Click ***OK***.

8. Close Internet Explorer.

Exercise 6.3	Install, Manage, and Remove a Sandbox Solution
Overview	In the following exercise, you will install and then remove a sandbox solution.
Completion time	10 minutes

1. Open Internet Explorer and go to *http://StudentXX*.

2. Click *Site Actions* and then click *Site Settings*. The Site Settings page displays.

3. In the *Galleries* section, click *Solutions*. The Solutions tab displays.

4. On the Ribbon, click the *Solutions* tab.

5. On the Ribbon, click *Upload Solution*. The Upload Document dialog displays.

6. In the Upload Document dialog box, click *Browse.* Then browse to the \\rwdc01\downloads\PrintList.wsp and click *Open*.

7. In the Upload Document dialog box, click *OK*. The Solution Gallery – Activate Solution page displays.

8. On the Ribbon, click *Activate* to activate the solution.

9. Open *Central Administration*.

10. Click *Application Management*, and then in the *Site Collections* section, click *Configure quotas and locks*. The Quotas and Locks page displays.

11. Select the *http://StudentXX* site collection.

12. In the *Site Quota Information* section, you can set the *Limit maximum usage per day to* settings based on a point total that you determine.

Question 1	What is the default individual limit maximum usage per day?

13. Click *OK*.

14. Close *Central Administration*.

15. Open Internet Explorer and go to *http://StudentXX*.

16. Click *Site Actions* and then select *Site Settings*. The Site Settings page displays.

17. In the *Galleries* section, click *Solutions*. The Solutions tab displays.

18. Click the check box next to *PrintList*. On the Ribbon, click *Deactivate*.

19. When the Solution Gallery – Deactivate Solution page displays, click *Deactivate*.

20. Click the check box next to *PrintListPackage*. On the Ribbon, click *Delete*.

21. When you are prompted to send the item to the Recycle Bin, click *OK*.

Exercise 6.4	Enable the Developer Dashboard
Overview	In the following exercise, you will enable the Developer Dashboard so that it can be used to troubleshoot the performance of a page opening in SharePoint.
Completion time	10 minutes

1. Click *Start* > *All Programs* > *Accessories*. Then right-click *Command Prompt* and select *Run as administrator*.

2. At the command prompt, change to the *C:\Program Files\Common files\Microsoft Shared\Web Server Extensions\14\Bin* folder.

3. To enable Developer Dashboard, execute the following command at the command prompt:

   ```
   stsadm -o setproperty -pn developer-dashboard -pv On
   ```

4. Open Internet Explorer and go to *http://StudentXX*. Notice the Developer Dashboard at the bottom of the screen.

5. To disable Developer Dashboard, execute the following command at the command prompt:

   ```
   stsadm -o setproperty -pn developer-dashboard -pv Off
   ```

6. Close the command prompt window.

LAB CHALLENGE: USE POWERSHELL TO DEPLOY AND REMOVE SOLUTIONS

Completion time	10 minutes

Using PowerShell, install and deploy \\rwdc01\downloads\sharepointlogger.wsp. After it is deployed, use PowerShell to uninstall and remove the sharepointlogger.wsp solution.

LAB 7
MANAGING ACCOUNTS AND USER ROLES

THIS LAB CONTAINS THE FOLLOWING EXERCISES AND ACTIVITIES:

Exercise 7.1   Manage SharePoint 2010 Administrators

Exercise 7.2   Manage Permission Levels

Exercise 7.3   Manage Site, List, and Library Permissions

Exercise 7.4   Create a Managed Account

Lab Challenge   Manage Active Directory and SharePoint 2010 Groups

BEFORE YOU BEGIN

The lab environment consists of student workstations connected to a local area network, along with a server that functions as the domain controller for a domain called contoso.com. The computers required for this lab are listed in Table 7-1.

Table 7-1
Computers required for Lab 7

Computer	Operating System	Computer Name
Instructor Server	Windows Server 2008 R2	RWDC01
Student Server	Windows Server 2008 R2	Student*xx, where xx* is your Student number.

> **NOTE**
>
> *In a classroom lab or virtual lab environment, there will be one classroom server and the students will have workstations named using consecutive numbers in place of the XX variable.*

In addition to the computers, you will also need the software listed in Table 7-2 in order to complete Lab 7.

Table 7-2
Software required for Lab 7

Software	Location
Lab 7 student worksheet	Lab07_worksheet.rtf (provided by instructor)

Working with Lab Worksheets

Each lab in this manual requires that you answer questions, shoot screen shots, and perform other activities that you will document in a worksheet named for the lab (such as Lab07_worksheet.rtf). Your instructor will provide you with access to the worksheets. It is recommended that you use a USB flash drive to store your worksheets, so you can submit them to your instructor for review. As you perform the exercises in each lab, open the appropriate worksheet file using WordPad, fill in the required information, and then save the file to your flash drive.

SCENARIO

Your manager wants you to review the administrative roles used in SharePoint, and the Sales Manager would like you to create a Sales site to be used by the sales team. In this lab, you will perform these tasks and then you will configure the Sales site so that only the sales staff can access the site.

After completing this lab, you will be able to:

- Add and remove the administrators at various levels of SharePoint

- Create, modify, and remove permission levels.

- Assign permission and permission levels to a user

- Create managed accounts

- Create and use Active Directory and SharePoint groups

Estimated lab time: 60 minutes

Exercise 7.1	Manage SharePoint 2010 Administrators
Overview	In the following exercise, you will manage different levels of administrators used within the SharePoint farm.
Completion time	15 minutes

1.   On your student server, log in as *contoso\Studentxx* (*xx* represents your student number) and use *Pa$$w0rd* as the password.

2.   Open *Central Administration* and click *Security*. The Security page displays.

3.   In the *Users* section, click *Manage the farm administrators group*. The People and Groups – Farm Administrators page displays.

4.   To add a user, click the *New* drop-down arrow and select *Add Users*. The Grant Permissions dialog box displays.

5.   Type *contoso\administrator* and then click *OK*.

6.   In Central Administration, click *Application Management*. The Application Management page displays.

7.   In the *Service Applications* section, click *Manage service applications*. The Manage Service Application Windows displays.

8.   In the *Type* column, click *User Profile Service Application* to highlight the row. Then in the Ribbon, on the *Service Applications* tab, click *Administrators*. The Administrators page displays.

9.   In the *To add an account, or group, type or select it below and click 'Add'* text box, type *contoso\administrators*. Click *Add* and then select *Full Control*.

10.   Click *OK*.

11.   Click *Security*.

12.   Click *Manage the farm administrators group*.

13.   To remove the administrator from the farm administrators group, click the *Administrator* check box. Then open the *Actions* menu and select *Remove Users from Group*.

14.   When you are prompted to remove these members, click *OK*.

15.   Click *Application Management*.

16. In the *Service Applications* section, click *Manage service applications*.

17. In the *Type* column, click *User Profile Service Application* to highlight the row. Then on the Ribbon, on the *Service Applications* tab, click *Administrators*. The Administrators page displays.

18. Click the *Administrators* group and then click *Remove*.

19. Click *OK* to close the Administrators for User Profile Service Application page.

20. In Central Administration, click *Application Management*. The Application Management page displays.

21. Click *Change site collection administrators*.

22. To define a second site collection administrator, in the *Secondary Site Collection Administrators* text box, type *contoso\administrator* and then click *OK*.

23. Launch Internet Explorer and go to *http://StudentXX* (*XX* is your student number).

24. Click the *Site Actions* menu and select *Site Settings*.

25. In the *Users and Permissions* section, click *Site collection administrators*.

26. To make the contoso\administrator account a collection administrator, in the *Site Collection Administrators* text box, type *contoso\administrator* and then click *OK*.

27. On the Site Settings page, in the *Users and Permissions* section, click *Site permissions*.

28. Click *Classroom SharePoint Owners*.

Question 1	Who is the SharePoint owner?

29. At the top of the page, click *New*. In the *Users/Groups* box, type *contoso\administrators* and then click *Check Names*.

30. Deselect the *Send welcome e-mail to the new users* option.

31. Click *OK* to grant permission.

32. Close all Internet Explorer windows.

Exercise 7.2   Manage Permission Levels

Overview	In the following exercise, you will create and manage the permission levels in SharePoint.
Completion time	20 minutes

1.   Click *Start* > *Administrative Tools* > *Active Directory* > *Users and Computers*.

2.   Expand the *contoso.com* domain.

3.   Right-click the *contoso.com* domain, click *New*, and then select *Organizational Unit*.

4.   In the *Name* box, type *StudentXX* and then click *OK*.

5.   Right-click the *StudentXX* OU, click *New*, and then select *User*. The new Object – User dialog box displays.

6.   Type the following information:

     First name: *User*

     Last Name: *XX* (*XX* is your student number).

     User logon name: *UserXX* (*XX* is your student number)

     User logon name (pre-Windows 2000): *UserXX* (*XX* is your student number).

7.   Click *Next*.

8.   In the *Password* text box and the *Confirm password* text box, type *Pa$$w0rd*. Select the *Password never expires* option.

9.   When a pop-up box displays, prompting you to confirm that you specified that the password should never expire, click *OK*. Click *Next*.

10. Click *Finish* to create the user.

11. Close *Active Directory Users and Computers*.

12. Launch Internet Explorer and go to *http://StudentXX* (*XX* is your student number).

13. Click the *Site Actions* menu and select *Site Permissions*.

14. On the Ribbon, click *Grant Permissions*.

15. In the *Select Users* text box, type *User XX*. The Permissions dialog box displays.

16. Select the ***Grant users permission directly*** option.

17. Select ***Full Control***.

18. Deselect the ***Send welcome e-email to the new users*** option.

19. Click ***OK***.

20. On the Ribbon, click ***Permission Levels***. The Permissions Levels page displays.

21. Click ***Add a Permission Level***.

22. In the ***Name*** text box, type ***Basic Permissions***.

23. Select the following permissions:

    List Permissions
    - ***Manage Lists***
    - ***Add Items***
    - ***Delete Items***
    - ***View Items*** (should already be checked)
    - ***Open Items***
    - ***View Versions***

24. Click ***Create***.

25. On the Ribbon, click ***Permission Levels***.

26. Select the ***User XX*** check box.

27. Click ***Edit User Permissions***. The Edit Permissions box displays.

28. Deselect the ***Full Control*** permission and select ***Basic Permissions***. Click ***OK***.

29. At the top of the page, click ***Permissions Levels***.

30. Select the ***Basic Permissions*** check box.

31. Click ***Delete Selected Permission Levels***. When you are prompted to confirm this action, click ***OK***.

32. Close Internet Explorer.

Exercise 7.3	Manage Site, List, and Library Permissions
Overview	In the following exercise, you will manage the site, list, and library permissions (including controlling if a site, list, or library permissions inherit permissions).
Completion time	15 minutes

1.   Launch Internet Explorer and go to ***http://StudentXX*** (*XX* is your student number).

2.   Click the ***Site Actions*** menu and choose ***New Site***.

3.   In the ***Title*** text box, type ***Level2***.

4.   In the ***URL Name:*** text box, type ***Level2*** (so the entire URL name should display ***http://StudentXX/Level2***).

5.   In the ***Template Selection*** section, on the Collaboration tab, choose ***Team Site***.

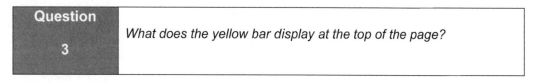

Question 2	For Permissions, what is the default value?

6.   Click ***Create***. When the site is created, you should be on the Level2 site.

7.   Click ***Site Actions*** and then select ***Site Permissions***.

8.   On the Ribbon, click ***Stop Inheriting Permissions***.

9.   When you are prompted to confirm that you are about to create unique permissions for this Web site, click ***OK***.

Question 3	What does the yellow bar display at the top of the page?

10.   On the Ribbon, click ***Inherit Permissions***.

11.   When you are prompted to continue, click ***OK***.

Question 4	What does the yellow bar display at the top of the page?

12.   Using Internet Explorer, go to ***http://StudentXX/Level2***.

13.   In the ***Libraries*** section, click the ***Shared Documents*** link.

14.   On the Ribbon, in the ***Library Tools*** group, click the ***Library*** tab.

15. On the Ribbon, in the *Settings* group, click *Library Permissions*.

16. On the Ribbon, click *Stop Inheriting Permissions*.

17. When you are prompted to confirm that you are creating unique permissions, click *OK*.

18. On the Ribbon, click *Check Permissions*.

19. In the *User/Group* text box, type *User XX* and then click *Check Now*.

Question 5	What are the permissions granted to User XX?

20. Click *Close*.

21. Close Internet Explorer.

Exercise 7.4	Use Managed Accounts
Overview	In the following exercise, you will create a service account in Active Directory and then create a managed account in SharePoint based on the service account.
Completion time	10 minutes

1. Click *Start* > *Administrative Tools* > *Active Directory* > *Users and Computers*.

2. Expand the *contoso.com* domain.

3. Right-click the *StudentXX* organizational unit, click *New*, and then select *User*. The new Object – User dialog box displays.

4. Enter the following information:

   - First name: *SPAdmin*
   - Last Name: *XX* (*XX* is your student number).
   - User logon name: *SPADMINXX* (*XX* is your student number)
   - User logon name (pre-Windows 2000): *SPAdminXX* (*XX* is your student number).
5. Click *Next*.

6. In the *Password* text box and the *Confirm password* text box, type *Pa$$w0rd*. Select the *Password never expires* option.

7. When a pop-up box displays, prompting you to confirm that you specified that the password should never expire, click *OK*. Click *Next*.

8. Click *Finish* to create the user.

9. Close *Active Directory Users and Computers*.

10. Open *Central Administration*.

11. Click *Security*.

12. In the *General Security* section, click *Configure managed accounts*. The Managed Accounts page displays.

13. Click *Register Managed Account*. The Registered Managed Account page displays.

14. In the Account Registration section, type *contoso\SPAdmin*.

15. In the *Password* text box, type *Pa$w0rd.*

16. In the *Automatic Password Change* section, select the *Enable automatic password change* check box.

17. Select the *Weekly* option.

18. Click *OK*.

LAB CHALLENGE: MANAGING ACTIVE DIRECTORY AND SHAREPOINT GROUPS

Completion time	15 minutes

In the StudentXX organizational unit, create a group called ADGroupXX that contains the UserXX. Also in SharePoint, create a group called SPGroup, which also contains UserXX. Then assign the contribute permission to the Level1 Shared Documents.

LAB 8
CONFIGURING SERVICE APPLICATIONS

THIS LAB CONTAINS THE FOLLOWING EXERCISES AND ACTIVITIES:

Exercise 8.1   Configure an Excel Services Application

Exercise 8.2   Manage InfoPath Forms Services

Exercise 8.3   Configure and Manage User Profiles

Exercise 8.4   Configure My Sites

BEFORE YOU BEGIN

The lab environment consists of student workstations connected to a local area network, along with a server that functions as the domain controller for a domain called contoso.com. The computers required for this lab are listed in Table 8-1.

Table 8-1
Computers required for Lab 8

Computer	Operating System	Computer Name
Instructor Server	Windows Server 2008 R2	RWDC01
Student Server	Windows Server 2008 R2	Studentxx, where xx is your Student number.

> **NOTE**
>
> *In a classroom lab or virtual lab environment, there will be one classroom server and the students will have workstations named using consecutive numbers in place of the XX variable.*

In addition to the computers, you will also need the software listed in Table 8-2 in order to complete Lab 8.

Table 8-2
Software required for Lab 8

Software	Location
Lab 8 student worksheet	Lab08_worksheet.rtf (provided by instructor)

Working with Lab Worksheets

Each lab in this manual requires that you answer questions, shoot screen shots, and perform other activities that you will document in a worksheet named for the lab (such as Lab08_worksheet.rtf). Your instructor will provide you with access to the worksheets. It is recommended that you use a USB flash drive to store your worksheets, so you can submit them to your instructor for review. As you perform the exercises in each lab, open the appropriate worksheet file using WordPad, fill in the required information, and save the file to your flash drive.

SCENARIO

Thus far, you have created sites for each department and have trained users to upload documents and create lists. However, your manager wants you to expand the capabilities of SharePoint by integrating Microsoft Word, Excel, Access, and InfoPath. In addition, your manager would like for SharePoint to display user information about users, such as what office they work in and their contact information. Lastly, your manager would like you to create individual sites for users.

After completing this lab, you will be able to:

■ Configure the Excel Services Application service application

■ Manage InfoPaths Forms Services

■ Establish User Profile Synchronization

■ Configure My Sites

Estimated lab time: 70 minutes

Exercise 8.1	Configure an Excel Service Application
Overview	In the following exercise, you will create and configure an Excel Service Application.
Completion time	15 minutes

1. On your student server, log in as *contoso\Studentxx* (*xx* represents your student number) and use *Pa$$w0rd* as the password.

2. Open *Central Administration*.

3. In the *Application Manager* section, click *Manage service applications*.

4. In the *Type* section, click *Excel Services Application Web Service Application* to highlight the Excel Services Application.

5. On the Ribbon, click *Delete*.

6. When the Delete Service Application page displays, select *Delete data associated with the Service Application* and click *OK*.

7. When the service application has been deleted, click *OK*.

8. On the Ribbon, click *New* and then click *Excel Services Application*.

9. In the *Name* text box, type *Excel Services Application*.

10. Select *Create new application pool*.

11. For the *Application pool name* text box, type *ExcelAppPool*.

12. For the configurable, select the *SPAdminXX* account that you created in Lab 7.

13. Click *OK*.

14. Click the *Excel Services Application* link.

15. Click *Global Settings*.

Question 1	Is encrypted communication required for client computers and front-end components of the Excel Services Application?

Question 2	What is the maximum sessions per user?

16. Click *OK* to close the Excel Services Application Settings page.

17. Click *Trusted File Locations*.

Question 3	*What is the default trusted file location?*

18. Click the *Add Trusted File Location* option.

19. In the *Address* text box, type *\\rwdc01\downloads*.

20. For the *Location* type, select *UNC*.

21. Select the *Children trusted* check box.

22. At the bottom of the page, click *OK*.

23. Close Internet Explorer.

Exercise 8.2	Manage InfoPath Forms Services
Overview	In the following exercise, you will configure InfoPath Forms Services, including activating and deactivating forms.
Completion time	15 minutes

1. Open *Central Administration*.

2. Click *General Application Settings*.

3. In the *InfoPath Forms Services* section, click *Manage form templates*.

4. At the end of the list, click *reviewpublishing_1033.xsn* and then click *Activate to a Site Collection*.

5. When the Active Form Template page displays, click *OK*.

6. Click *reviewpublishing_1033.xsn* and then select *Quiesce Form Template*.

7. To specify 1 minute, in *The form template should be fully quiesced after this long* text box, type*1*. Click *Start Quiescing*.

Question 4	*What is the status of Quiesce?*

8. After approximately 90 seconds, click **Refresh**.

Question 5	What is the status of Quiesce?

9. Click **Cancel**.

Question 6	What is the status of Quiesce?

10. Click **reviewpublishing_1033.xsn** and then click **Quiesce Form Template**.

11. Click **Reset Template**.

12. Click **Cancel**.

Question 7	What is the status of the review publishing_1036.xsn template?

13. On the Manage Form Templates page, click **reviewpublishing_1033.xsn** and then select **Deactivate from a Site Collection**.

14. On the Deactivate Form Template page, click **OK**.

15. On the manage Form Templates page, click the **reveiwpublishing_1033.xsn** and click **Activate to a Site Collection**.

16. On the Activate Form Template page, click **OK**.

17. In Central Administration, click **General Applications Settings**.

18. In the **InfoPath Forms Services** section, click **Configure InfoPath Forms Services**.

Question 8	What options are enabled for the User Browser-Enabled Form Templates?

19. Click **OK** to close the Configure InfoPath Forms Services page.

20. Leave the system logged in for the next exercise.

Exercise 8.3   Configure and Manage User Profiles

Overview	In the following exercise, you will synchronize Active Directory information to SharePoint user profiles.
Completion time	30 minutes

1. Click *Start > Administrative Tools > Active Directory Users and Computers*.

2. Right-click *contoso.com* and select *Delegate Control*.

3. When the wizard begins, click *Next*.

4. Click *Add*.

5. In the *Select Users, Computers, or Groups* option, type *SPAdminXX*. Click *OK*.

6. On the *Users or Groups* page, click *Next*.

7. Select *Create a Custom Task* and then click *Next*.

8. When you are prompted for the Active Directory Object Type, leave the default selection and then click *Next*.

9. When the Permissions page displays, select the *Replicating Directory Changes* permission and then click *Next*.

10. Click *Finish*.

11. Open *Central Administration*.

12. In the *Application Management* section, click *Manage Service Applications*.

13. Verify that *User Profile Service Application* exists.

14. Click *System Settings* and then click *Manage services on this server*.

15. Next to *User Profile Synchronization Services*, click the *Start* button

16. Type the password for the *StudentXX* account and then click *OK*.

17. The Profile Synchronization Service will start after 5-10 minutes. While you are waiting, click *Start > Administrative Tools > Internet Information Services (IIS) Manager*.

18. Expand the *StudentXX* server.

19. Right-click the *StudentXX* server and select *Stop*. Then right-click the *StudentXX* server and select *Start*. Close *Internet Information Services (IIS) Manager*.

20. After the User Profile Synchronization Services is started, in the *Application Management* section, click *Manage Service Applications*. The Manage Service Applications page displays.

21. Click the *User Profile Service Application* link. The User Profile Service Application page displays.

22. In the *Synchronization* section, click *Configure Synchronization Connections*. The Synchronization Connections page displays.

23. Click *Create New Connection*.

24. In the *Connection Name* text box, type *Active Directory Connection*.

25. In the *Connection Settings* section, in the *Forest name* text box, type *contoso.com*.

26. In the *Containers* section, click *Populate Containers*.

27. When the *contoso.com* domain shows, click *Select All*.

28. Click *OK*.

29. When the connection is created, click *Application Management*. Click *Manage service applications* and then click *User Profile Service Application*.

30. Click *Start Profile Synchronization*. The Start Profile Synchronization page displays.

31. Select *Start Full Synchronization* and then click *OK*.

32. In Internet Explorer, click the *Refresh* button to refresh the page. Notice the Profile Synchronization Status and Current Synchronization Stage.

33. Keep refreshing the page until the synchronization is done (as indicated when the *Profile Synchronization Status* is *Idle*).

34. Click *Configure Synchronization Timer Job*.

Question 9	*How often does User Profile Incremental Synchronization occur?*

35. Click *OK*.

36. Leave the system logged in for the next exercise.

Exercise 8.4	Configure My Sites
Overview	In the following exercise, you will create a site collection to host My Sites and then you will configure My Sites, which will allow users to their own personal sites within SharePoint.
Completion time	10 minutes

1. Open *Central Administration*.

2. Click *Application Management* and then click *Create site collections*. The Create Site Collection page displays.

3. Make sure that the *http://StudentXX/* Web application is selected. If *http://StudentXX/* is not selected, click the current Web Application and then click *Change Web Application*. Then double-click *SharePoint - 80*.

4. In the *Title* text box, type *MY SITES*.

5. In the *Web Site Address* section, in the *URL* text box, type *MySites*. The address should display *http://StudentXX/my/personal/MySites*.

6. In the *Template Selection* section, click the *Enterprise* tab and then click *My Site Host*.

7. In the *Primary Site Collection* text box, type *contoso\StudentXX*.

8. In the *Secondary Site Collection Administrator* text box, type *contoso\SPAdminXX*.

9. Click *OK* to create the site collection.

10. When the site collection is created, click *OK*.

11. Click *Application Management* and then click *Manage Web applications*. The Web Applications page displays.

12. Select *SharePoint - 80*.

13. In the Security group, click *Self-Service Site Creation*. The Self-Service Site Collection Management dialog box displays.

14. With the Enable Self-Service Site Creation set to *On*, click *OK*.

15. Click *Application Management* and then, in the *Service Applications* section, click *Manage Service Application*.

16. Click the *User Profile Service Application*. The Manage Profile Service page displays.

17. In the *My Site Settings* section, click *Setup My Sites*. My Site Settings page displays.

18. Review the default settings and then click *OK*.

19. Close Internet Explorer.

LAB 9
CONFIGURING INDEXES AND SEARCHES

THIS LAB CONTAINS THE FOLLOWING EXERCISES AND ACTIVITIES:

Exercise 9.1   Create and Configure the Search Service Application

Exercise 9.2   Create and Manage Content Crawls

Exercise 9.3   Create and Manage a Search Center Site

Lab Challenge   Install and Enable a TIFF IFilter

BEFORE YOU BEGIN

The lab environment consists of student workstations connected to a local area network, along with a server that functions as the domain controller for a domain called contoso.com. The computers required for this lab are listed in Table 9-1.

Table 9-1
Computers required for Lab 9

Computer	Operating System	Computer Name
Instructor Server	Windows Server 2008 R2	RWDC01
Student Server	Windows Server 2008 R2	Studentxx, *where xx* is your Student number.

In addition to the computers, you will also need the software listed in Table 9-2 in order to complete Lab 9.

Table 9-2
Software required for Lab 9

Software	Location
Lab 9 student worksheet	Lab09_worksheet.rtf (provided by instructor)

Working with Lab Worksheets

Each lab in this manual requires that you answer questions, shoot screen shots, and perform other activities that you will document in a worksheet named for the lab (such as Lab09_worksheet.rtf). Your instructor will provide you with access to the worksheets. It is recommended that you use a USB flash drive to store your worksheets, so you can submit them to your instructor for review. As you perform the exercises in each lab, open the appropriate worksheet file using WordPad, fill in the required information, and then save the file to your flash drive.

SCENARIO

As users add documents and create lists, they're complaining that it's difficult to find items. Therefore, they are looking for you to create or configure a search solution so they can find items more quickly.

After completing this lab, you will be able to:

- Create and configure the Search Service Application

- Create and manage content crawls

- Create and search for content

- Install and enable a TIFF IFilter

Estimated lab time: 65 minutes

Exercise 9.1	Create and Configure the Search Service Application
Overview	In this exercise, you will create a search service account and a Search Service Application.
Completion time	15 minutes

1. On your student server, log in as ***contoso\Studentxx*** (*xx* represents your student number) and use ***Pa$$w0rd*** as the password.

2. Click ***Start*** > ***Administrative Tools*** > ***Active Directory Users and Computers***.

3. If necessary, expand the ***contoso.com*** domain.

4. Right-click the ***StudentXX*** organizational unit (OU), click ***New***, and then choose ***User***.

5. In the ***Full Name*** text box and ***User logon*** text box, type ***SharePointSearchXX***, and then click ***Next***.

6. In the ***Password*** text box and the ***Confirm password*** text box, type ***Pa$w0rd***. Choose ***Password never expires***.

7. When you are prompted to confirm your selection that the password should never expire, click ***OK***. Click ***Next***.

8. Click ***Finish*** to create the user.

9. Open ***Central Administration***.

10. Launch Internet Explore and go to ***http://StudentXX***.

11. Click the ***Site Actions*** menu and select ***Site Settings***.

12. In the ***Users and Permissions*** section, click ***Site collection administrators***.

13. To allow the SharePoint SearchXX account to have access to the SharePoint sites, add ***contoso\SharePointSearchXX*** to the list of Site Collection Administrators. Click ***OK***.

14. Close the Internet Explorer window that hosts the ***http://StudentXX*** Web site.

15. Open ***Central Administration***.

16. In the ***Application Management*** section, in the ***Service Applications*** section, click ***Manage service applications***. The Manage Service Application page displays.

17. Click ***Search Service Application***. In the ***Type*** column, highlight the Search Service Application.

18. On the Ribbon, click ***Delete***.

19. Select ***Delete data associated with the Service Application connections*** and then click ***OK***.

20. When the Service Application is deleted, click ***OK***.

21. On the Ribbon, click *New*, and then click *Search Service Application*. The Create New Search Service Application page displays.

22. Click *Register new managed account*. The Register New Managed Account page displays.

23. In the *User name* text box, type *contoso\SharePointSearchXX*. In the *Password* text box, type *Pa$$w0rd*.

24. Click *OK* to accept your settings and return to the Create New Search Service Application page.

25. For the *Search Service Account* setting, select *contoso\SharePointSearchXX* and then click *OK*.

26. In the *Application Pool for Search Admin Web Service* section, select *Use existing application pool* and then select the *SearchAppPool*.

27. In the *Application Pool for Search Query and Site Settings Web Service* section, select *Use existing application pool* and then select *SearchAppPool*.

28. Click *OK* to accept your settings and create the new Search Service Application.

29. When the Search Service Application has been created, click *OK*.

30. Back on the Manage Service Application page, click *Search Service Application*.

31. Click the link in the *Default content access account* row. The Default Content Access Account page displays.

32. In the Default Content Access Account dialog box, in the *Account* text box, type *contoso\SharePointSearchXX* with the password of *Pa$w0rd*. Click *OK*.

33. Leave the computer logged on for the next exercise.

Exercise 9.2	Create and Manage Content Crawls
Overview	Using the previously created search application service, in this lab, you will crawl your SharePoint site.
Completion time	20 minutes

1. Open *Central Administration*.

2. In the *Application Management* section, click *Manage service applications*. The Manage Service Application page displays.

3. Click the *Search Service Application*. The Search Administration page displays.

4. In the *Crawling* section, click *Content Sources*. The Manage Content Sources page displays.

Question 1	What content sources are already created?

5. Click *Local SharePoint sites*.

Question 2	What are the Start Addresses?

6. At the bottom of the page, click *Cancel*.

7. Right-click *Local SharePoint Sites* and select *Start Full Crawl*.

8. After about 15 seconds, click the *Refresh* link. Then occasionally click the *Refresh* button until the crawl is done.

Question 3	How long did the crawl take?

9. When the crawl is done, click *Start Incremental Crawl*.

10. After about 15 seconds, click the *Refresh* link. Then occasionally click the *Refresh* button until the crawl is done.

Question 4	How long did the incremental crawl take?

11. Click *Local SharePoint sites*.

Question 5	What is the crawl schedule for full crawls and incremental crawls?

12. In the *Crawl Schedules* section, click *Create schedule for the Full Crawl*. The Manage Schedules page displays.

13. Configure the crawl to run once a day starting at *1:00 AM* and then click *OK*.

14. In the *Crawl Schedules* section, click *Create schedule for the Incremental Crawl*. The Manage Schedules page displays.

15. Configure the crawl will repeat every *15 minutes* starting at *1:00 AM* and then click *OK*.

16. Click *OK* to accept your settings and close the Edit Content Source page.

17. Click *Start all crawls*.

18. When the crawls are completed, in the *Crawling* section, click *Crawler Impact Rules*. The Crawler Impact Rules page displays.

19. Click *Add Rule*. The Add Crawler Impact rule page displays.

20. Type *StudentXX* (without typing the http://protocol).

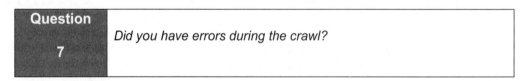

Question 6	What is the default for simultaneous requests?

21. Click *OK* to accept your settings and close the Add Crawler Impact Rule page.

22. Click *Application Management* and then click *Manage service applications*.

23. Click *Search Service Application*.

24. In the *Crawling* section, click *File Types*.

25. Click *New File Type*.

26. In the *File extension* text box, type *pdf*.

27. Click *OK*.

28. In the *Administration* section, click *Search Administration*.

Question 7	Did you have errors during the crawl?

29. In the *Crawling* section, click *Crawl Log*.

30. Click *Local SharePoint sites*.

31. At the top of the page, click *Error Message*.

32. Click *View*.

33. Close *Internet Explorer*.

34. Leave the computer logged in for the next exercise.

Exercise 9.3	Create and Manage a Search Center Site
Overview	In the following exercise, you will create a dedicated search center site. You will then perform several searches looking for content.
Completion time	20 minutes

1. Open *Central Administration*.

2. In the *Application Management* section, click *Create site collections*.

3. In the *Title* text box, type *Search Center Site*.

4. In the *Web Site Address* section, click the drop-down, select */sites/*, and then type *Search* in the text box to complete the URL.

5. In the *Template Selection* section, click the *Enterprise* tab and then choose the *Enterprise Search Center* template.

6. In the *Primary Site Collection Administrator* section, in the *User name* text box, type *contoso\StudentXX*.

7. In the *Secondary Site Collection Administrator* section, in the *User name* text box, type *contoso\SharePointSearchXX*.

8. Click *OK*.

9. Launch Internet Explorer and go to *http://StudentXX/Search*.

10. Click the *Site Actions* menu and then click *Site Settings*.

11. In the Users and Permissions section, click *People and groups*.

12. Click *Enterprise Search Center Visitors*.

13. Click the *New* menu and then choose *Add Users*.

14. In the Users/Groups text box, type *NT Authority\authenticated users*.

15. Click *OK*.

16. Right-click the Windows desktop, click *New*, and then choose *Microsoft Word Document*.

17. Rename the document *SearchDoc.docx*.

18. Double-click *SearchDocx*.

19. On the first line, type your name.

20. On the second line, type *This is my sample SharePoint document*.

21. Save and close the document.

22. In Internet Explorer, go to *http://studentXX*.

23. In the *Libraries* section, click *Shared Documents*.

24. Click the *Add document* link.

25. Browse to your desktop and select the *SearchDoc.docx*. When you have specified the document, click *OK*.

26. In Internet Explorer, go to *http://StudentXX/Search.*

27. Search for *SharePoint is Awesome*.

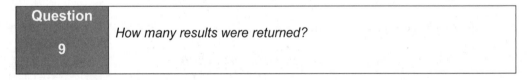

Question	How many results were returned?
8	

28. Open *Central Administration*.

29. Click *Manage service applications*.

30. Click *Search Service Application*.

31. Click *Content Sources*.

32. Click *Start all crawls*.

33. When the crawl is complete, return to the *http://StudentXX\Search* search page.

34. Search for *SharePoint is Awesome*.

Question	How many results were returned?
9	

35. In Internet Explorer, go to *http://StudentXX site*.

36. At the top of the window, search for *SharePoint is Awesome* and then click *Search*.

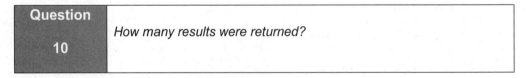

Question	How many results were returned?
10	

37. Leave the computer logged in for the next exercise.

LAB CHALLENGE: INSTALL AND ENABLE A TIFF IFILTER

Completion time	10 minutes

On the SharePoint server, install the TIFF IFilter and configure Windows to automatically read TIFF documents with the OCR.

LAB 10
MONITORING AND ANALYZING THE SHAREPOINT ENVIRONMENT

THIS LAB CONTAINS THE FOLLOWING EXERCISES AND ACTIVITIES:

Exercise 10.1	Configure and Manage SharePoint Logging
Exercise 10.2	Use SharePoint Health Analyzer
Exercise 10.3	Configure Usage and Health Data Collection
Exercise 10.4	Manage Timer Jobs
Exercise 10.5	Configure Quotas
Exercise 10.6	Configure Locks
Exercise 10.7	Configure Output Caching, Object Caching, and IIS Compression

BEFORE YOU BEGIN

The lab environment consists of student workstations connected to a local area network, along with a server that functions as the domain controller for a domain called contoso.com. The computers required for this lab are listed in Table 10-1.

Table 10-1
Computers required for Lab 10

Computer	Operating System	Computer Name
Instructor Server	Windows Server 2008 R2	RWDC01
Student Server	Windows Server 2008 R2	Student*xx, where xx* is your Student number.

> **NOTE**
> *In a classroom lab or virtual lab environment, there will be one classroom server and the students will have workstations named using consecutive numbers in place of the XX variable.*

In addition to the computers, you will also need the software listed in Table 10-2 in order to complete Lab 10.

Table 10-2
Software required for Lab 10

Software	Location
Lab 10 student worksheet	Lab10_worksheet.rtf (provided by instructor)

Working with Lab Worksheets

Each lab in this manual requires that you answer questions, shoot screen shots, and perform other activities that you will document in a worksheet named for the lab (such as Lab10_worksheet.rtf). Your instructor will provide you with access to the worksheets. It is recommended that you use a USB flash drive to store your worksheets, so you can submit them to your instructor for review. As you perform the exercises in each lab, open the appropriate worksheet file using WordPad, fill in the required information, and then save the file to your flash drive.

SCENARIO

From time to time, users have reported that SharePoint has been slow from time to time. Therefore, you need to look at the SharePoint logs and other available tools looking for problems. In addition, you need to confirm if Output caching and object caching is enabled.

After completing this lab, you will be able to:

- Analyze the SharePoint logs

- Use SharePoint Health Analyzer to quickly view problems or potential problems

- Enable Usage and Health Data Collection to look at SharePoint performance

- Manage timer jobs

- Configure Quotas and Locks

- Enable caching and IIS compression

Estimated lab time: 80 minutes

Exercise 10.1	Configure and Manage SharePoint Logging
Overview	In this exercise, you will access the SharePoint logs using PowerShell cmdlts and by Notepad. You will then configure the logging level for SharePoint.
Completion time	30 minutes

1. On your student server, log in as *contoso\Studentxx* (*xx* represents your student number) and use *Pa$$w0rd* as the password.

2. Click *Start* > *All Programs* > *Microsoft SharePoint 2010 Products* > *SharePoint 2010 Management Shell*.

3. To view all trace events, execute the following command:

   Get-SPLogEvent

4. To display trace events by level (such as Error), execute the following command:

   Get-SPLogEvent | Where-Object {$_.Level -eq "Error"}

5. To display error entries from a one-hour period, execute a command to show the logs for the last hour: For example, to show the errors on 12/04/2011 from 5:00 p.m. to 6:00 p.m., execute the following command:

   Get-SPLogEvent -StartTime "12/04/2011 17:00" -EndTime "12/04/2011 18:00"

Question	
1	*What command did you execute?*

6. Click *Start* > *Computer*.

7. Navigate to the following folder:

   C:\Program Files\Common Files\Microsoft Shared\Web Server Extensions\14\LOGS

8.   Double-click the most recent log file (file with the *.log* filename extension). The log file will be opened in Notepad.

9.   Maximize the Notepad window so that displays in the entire screen.

10. In Notepad, click the *Format* menu and choose *Word Wrap*.

11. Click *Edit*, choose *Find*, and then search for *Error*. Review the error.

12. Click *Find Next* to see the next error. Review the errors located in the document.

13. After viewing all of the errors, close Notepad.

14. Close the Logs folder window.

15. Open *Central Administration*.

16. Click *Monitoring*. The Monitor page displays.

17. In the Reporting section, click *Configure Diagnostic Logging*. The Configure Diagnostic Logging page displays.

18. Expand the SharePoint Server category by clicking the plus sign (+) next to SharePoint Server.

Question 2	What is the default Event level and Trace Level for SharePoint Server?

19. Select the *SharePoint Server* check box.

20. Click the drop-down arrow under *Least critical event to report to the event log* and then choose *Verbose*.

21. Click the drop-down arrow under *Least critical event to report to the trace log* and then choose *Verbose*.

Question 3	What is the default path for the Trace Log?

Question 4	What is the number of days to store log files?

22. Select the ***Restrict Trace Log disk space usage*** check box and set the maximum trace log disk usage space to *5* GB.

23. Click ***OK***.

24. Click ***Start*** > ***All Programs*** > ***Microsoft SharePoint 2010 Products*** > ***SharePoint 2010 Management Shell***.

25. To view the trace severity levels, execute the following command:

    ```
    get-sploglevel |more
    ```

26. To configure PowerPoint to Verbose mode, execute the following command:

    ```
    set-sploglevel –eventseverity Error –identity powerpoint
    ```

27. To view the trace severity levels, execute the following command:

    ```
    get-sploglevel |more
    ```

28. Press and release the ***space bar*** repeatedly to look for PowerPoint to see the new status.

29. Continue pressing the ***space bar*** until you return to the command prompt.

30. Close the PowerShell command prompt window.

31. Go back to the ***Central Administration Monitoring*** page.

32. In the ***Reporting*** section, click ***Configure Diagnostic Logging***. The Configure Diagnostic Logging page displays.

33. Expand the SharePoint Server category by clicking the Plus sign (+) next to SharePoint Server.

Question 5	What is the default Event level and Trace Level for SharePoint Server?

34. Select the ***All Categories*** check box.

35. For the least critical event to report to the event log, select ***Information***.

36. For the least critical event to report to the trace log, select ***Medium***.

37. Click ***OK***.

38. Keep the system logged in for the next exercise.

Exercise 10.2	Use SharePoint Health Analyzer
Overview	In the following exercise, you will use SharePoint Health Analyzer to find problems and potential problems.
Completion time	5 minutes

1. Open *Central Administration*.

Question 6	How does SharePoint Health Analyzer show you that you have critical errors?

2. Click *Monitoring*. The Monitoring page displays.

3. In the *Health Analyzer* section, click *Review problems and solutions*. The Review Problems and Solutions page displays.

4. Review the current alerts. Click each error. Read the Explanation and Remedy.

5. In Central Administration, click *Monitoring*.

6. In the *Health Analyzer* section, click *Review rule definitions*. The Health Analyzer Rule Definitions page.

7. In the *Category: Performance* section, click the *Search - One or more crawl databases may have fragmented indices*. The Rule Definitions page displays.

8. On the Ribbon, click *Edit Item*. The Edit dialog page displays.

9. Change the schedule to *Weekly*.

10. Click *Save* to save changes and close the Health Analyze Rule Definition.

11. Leave the system logged in for the next exercise.

Exercise 10.3	Configure Usage and Health Data Collection
Overview	In the following exercise, you will make sure that usage and health data collection is enabled. You will then run various administrative reports.
Completion time	10 minutes

1. Open *Central Administration*.

2. Click *Monitoring*. The Monitoring page displays.

3. In the Reporting section, click *Configure usage and health data collection*. The Configure Web analytics and health data collection page displays.

Question 7	By default, are there any events or collections that are not enabled?

4.   At the bottom of the page, click *Cancel* to return to the Monitoring page.

5.   In the *Reporting* section, click the *View Web Analytics reports*. The Web Analytics Reports – Summary page displays.

Question 8	How many pages and how many unique visitors do you have for the SharePoint - 80?

6.   Click the *SharePoint – 80* Web application.

7.   On the left side of the page, click *Number of Page Views*.

8.   Click *Number of Daily Unique Visitors*

9.   Click *Top Pages*.

10.   Click *Top Visitors*.

11.   Click *Top Browsers*.

12.   Select *Number of Site Collections*.

13.   To view the Administrative Reports, click the *Customized Reports* link. The Administrative Report Library page displays.

14.   Click the *Search Administration reports* folder. The Search Administrative Report page displays.

15.   Click *CrawlRatePerContentSource*.

16.   Click Central Administration at the top of the screen.

17.   Click *Monitoring* to go to the Monitoring page.

18.   Leave the system logged in for the next exercise.

Exercise 10.4	Manage Timer Jobs
Overview	In the following exercise, you will see if any timer jobs are running. You will then modify a timer job.
Completion time	5 minutes

1.   Open *Central Administration*.

2.   Click *Monitoring*.

3.   To see when a job is scheduled to run next, in the *Timer Jobs* section, click *Check job status*. The Timer Job Status page displays.

4.   To see jobs that are currently running, in the *Timer Links* section, click *Running Jobs*. The Running Jobs page displays.

5.   To see a history of jobs, click *Job History*. The Job History page displays.

6.   To see the current timer jobs, click *Job Definitions*. The Job Definitions page displays.

Question	
9	*How often does the Audit Log Trimming run?*

7.   To modify the Audit Log Trimming job, click *Audit Log Trimming* for the *SharePoint – 80* Web application.

8.   Change the timer job schedule to *Weekly*.

9.   Click *OK*.

10.   Close Internet Explorer.

Exercise 10.5	Configure Quotas
Overview	In the following exercise, you will create a quota template and apply the template to a site collection.
Completion time	10 minutes

1.   Open *Central Administration*.

2.   Click *Application Management*.

3.   In the Site Collections section, click *Specify quota template*. The Quota Templates page displays.

4.   In the Template section, select *Create a new quota template*.

5.   In the *New template name* text box, type *Default*.

6. To limit the storage for the template, select ***Limit site storage to a maximum of*** and specify the size of ***4096*** MB.

7. To specify when a warning email is sent to the site collection administrator, specify a threshold of ***3500*** MB.

8. In the ***Sandboxed Solutions with Code Limits*** section, in the ***Limit the maximum usage per day to*** text box, type ***300***.

9. Deselect ***Send warning e-mail when usage per day reaches***.

10. Click ***OK***.

11. On the Application Management page, in the ***Site Collections*** section, click ***Quotas and Locks***. The Site Collection Quotas and Locks page displays.

12. Click the Site Collection and then click ***Change Site Collection***. Change the Web Application to ***http://StudentXX:80*** and then click ***OK***.

13. Change the current quota template to ***Default***.

14. Click ***OK***.

Exercise 10.6	Configuring Locks
Overview	In the following exercise, you will make a site collection read-only, then you make is read-write.
Completion time	10 minutes

1. Open ***Central Administration***.

2. Click ***Application Management***.

3. In the ***Site Collections*** section, click ***Quotas and Locks***. The Site Collection Quotas and Locks page displays.

4. Click the Site Collection and then click ***Change Site Collection***. Change the Web Application to ***http://StudentXX:80*** and then click ***OK***.

5. Select the ***Read-Only*** lock status.

6. In the ***Additional lock information*** text box, type ***Test*** and then click ***OK***.

7. Launch Internet Explorer and go to ***http://StudentXX***.

8. Click ***Shared Documents***.

9. Move the mouse pointer to ***SearchDoc*** and click the down arrow.

Question 10	Is there a Delete option?

10. Return to *Central Administration*.

11. On the *Application Management* page, in the *Site Collections* section, click *Quotas and Locks*. The Site Collection Quotas and Locks page displays.

12. Click the Site Collection and then click *Change Site Collection*. Change the Web Application to *http://StudentXX:80* and then click *OK*.

13. Select the *Not locked* status.

14. Return to *http://StudentXX Shared Documents*.

15. Refresh the screen by clicking the *Refresh* button.

16. Move the mouse pointer to *SearchDoc* and click the down arrow.

Question 11	Is there a Delete option?

17. Close all Internet Explorer windows.

Exercise 10.7	Configure Output Caching, Object Caching, and IIS Compression
Overview	In the following exercise, you will use Internet Information Services (IIS) Manager to optimize the performance of SharePoint.
Completion time	10 minutes

1. Click *Start > Administrative Tools > Internet Information Services (IIS) Manager*.

2. In the Connections pane, expand the *StudentXX* that hosts the Web application.

3. Expand the *Sites* container.

4. Right-click the *SharePoint – 80* Web site and then click *Explore*.

5. Press the *Alt* key to show the menus. Then click the *Tools* menu and choose *Folder Options*.

6.   Click the *View* tab.

7.   Select the ***Show hidden files, folders, or drives*** option.

8.   Click *OK* to accept your settings and close the Folder options dialog box.

9.   Right-click the ***Web.config*** file and then click *Open*.

10. Locate the line that begins with *<OutputCacheProfiles*.

11. Set the useCacheProfileOverrides attribute to ***true***.

12. Locate the line that begins with *<ObjectCache* and view the new value.

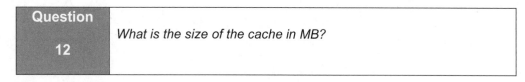

Question 12	What is the size of the cache in MB?

13. Save the ***Web.config*** file and close the text editor.

14. Close the Windows Explorer ***80*** folder.

15. With Internet Information Services (IIS) Manager open, click the ***StudentXX*** server.

16. If the ***Features view*** is not selected, select it.

17. In the ***IIS*** section, double-click ***Compression***. The Compression page displays.

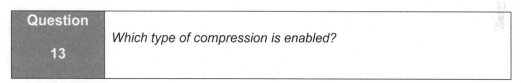

Question 13	Which type of compression is enabled?

18. Close Internet Information Services (IIS) Manager.

LAB 11
MANAGING AUTHENTICATION PROVIDERS

BEFORE YOU BEGIN

The lab environment consists of student workstations connected to a local area network, along with a server that functions as the domain controller for a domain called contoso.com. The computers required for this lab are listed in Table 11-1.

Table 11-1
Computers required for Lab 11

Computer	Operating System	Computer Name
Instructor Server	Windows Server 2008 R2	RWDC01
Student Server	Windows Server 2008 R2	Student*xx, where xx* is your Student number.

> **NOTE**
> *In a classroom lab or virtual lab environment, there will be one classroom server and the students will have workstations named using consecutive numbers in place of the XX variable.*

In addition to the computers, you will also need the software listed in Table 11-2 in order to complete Lab 11.

Table 11-2
Software required for Lab 11

Software	Location
Lab 11 student worksheet	Lab11_worksheet.rtf (provided by instructor)

Working with Lab Worksheets

Each lab in this manual requires that you answer questions, shoot screen shots, and perform other activities that you will document in a worksheet named for the lab (such as Lab11_worksheet.rtf). Your instructor will provide you with access to the worksheets. It is recommended that you use a USB flash drive to store your worksheets, so you can submit them to your instructor for review. As you perform the exercises in each lab, open the appropriate worksheet file using WordPad, fill in the required information, and then save the file to your flash drive.

SCENARIO

To this point, your SharePoint site has been using NTLM for authentication. Your manager has asked that you test other forms of authentication to see how difficult they are to set up and if there are any disadvantages after they are installed.

After completing this lab, you will be able to:

- Create a site collection that uses anonymous authentication. Create a site collection that uses Kerberos authentication. Create a site collection that uses Basic authentication.

- Create a site that uses Claims-Based authentication.

Estimated lab time: 60 minutes

Exercise 11.1	Configure Anonymous Access
Overview	In the following exercise, you create an application that will use Anonymous Access. You will then create a site collection for the Web application.
Completion time	15 minutes

1. On your student server, log in as ***contoso\Studentxx*** (*xx* represents your student number) and use ***Pa$$w0rd*** as the password.

2. Click ***Start***, right-click ***Computer***, and then select ***Manage***.

3. When Server Manager displays, expand ***Configuration***.

4. Expand ***Local users and Groups***.

5. Click ***Groups***.

6. Double-click ***Administrators***. The Administrators Properties dialog box displays.

7. Click ***Add***. The Select Users, Computers, Service Accounts, or Groups dialog box displays.

8. In the ***Enter the object names to select*** text box, type ***SPAdminXX***.

9. Click ***OK*** to accept your settings and close the Select Users, Computers, Service Accounts, or Groups.

10. Click ***OK*** to accept your settings and close the Administrators Properties.

11. Open ***Central Administration***.

12. Click ***Application Management***.

13. In the ***Web Applications*** section, click ***Manage Web Applications***. The Web Applications Management page displays.

14. On the Ribbon, click ***New***.

15. Change the port to ***2000***.

16. While the **Create new application pool** is selected, click the ***Configurable*** drop-down arrow and select the ***contoso\SPAdminXX*** account.

17. Click ***OK***.

18. When the application is created, click ***OK***.

19. Click ***Application Management***.

20. Click ***Create site collections***.

21. If necessary, change the Web application to ***http://StudentXX:2000***. If you need to change the Web application, click the current Web application and then click ***Change Web Application***. Click ***SharePoint – 2000***.

22. In the ***Title*** text box, type ***Anonymous***.

23. In the *Primary Site Collection Administrators* text box, type *contoso\StudentXX*.

24. In the *Secondary Site Collection Administrators* text box, type *contoso\SPAdminXX*

25. Click *OK* to accept your settings and create the site collection.

26. When the site collection is created, click *OK*.

27. Launch Internet Explorer and go to *http://StudentXX:2000*.

28. Click the *Site Actions* menu and then choose *Site Permissions*. The Permissions page displays.

29. On the Ribbon, click *Anonymous Access*. The Anonymous Access page displays.

30. Select *Entire Web site* and click *OK*.

31. Close Internet Explorer.

Exercise 11.2	Configure and Managing Kerberos
Overview	In the following exercise, you will configure the SPN for a service account. Then you will create a Web application that will use Kerberos and then you will create a site collection for the Web application that will support Kerberos.
Completion time	20 minutes

1. Click *Start > Administrative Tools > ADSI Edit*.

2. Right-click *ADSI Edit* in the console tree and then click *Connect To*.

3. When the Connection Settings dialog displays, click *OK*.

4. Expand *Default Naming Context* in the console tree, expand *contoso.com*, and then navigate to the *StudentXX* OU, where the SPAdminXX user account is.

5. In the Details pane, right-click the *SPAdminXX* account and then choose *Properties*.

6. In the *Attributes* list, double-click *servicePrincipalName* to display the Multi-valued String Editor dialog.

7. In the *Value to add* field, type *HTTP/StudentXX:2001* and then click *Add*.

8. Click *OK* to accept your settings and close the Multi-Valued String Editor dialog box.

9. Click *OK* to accept your settings and close the user properties.

10. Close *ASDI Edit*.

11. Open *Central Administration*.

12. Click *Application Management*.

13. In the *Web Applications* section, click *Manage Web Applications*. The Web Applications Management page displays.

14. On the Ribbon, click *New*.

15. Change the port to *2001*.

16. In the Security Configuration section, for the *Authentication provider* setting, select *Negotiate (Kerberos)*.

17. While the *Create new application pool* is selected, click the *Configurable* drop-down arrow and select the *contoso\SPAdminXX* account.

18. Click *OK*.

19. When you are prompted to confirm that you want to use Kerberos authentication, click *OK*.

20. When the application is created, click *OK*.

21. Click *Application Management*.

22. Click *Create site collections*.

23. If necessary, change the Web application to *http://StudentXX:2001*. If you need to change the Web application, click the current Web application and then click *Change Web Application*. Click *SharePoint – 2001*.

24. In the *Title* text box, type *Kerberos*.

25. In the *Primary Site Collection Administrators* section, type *contoso\StudentXX*.

26. In the *Secondary Site Collection Administrators* section, type *contoso\SPAdminXX.*

27. Click *OK* to accept your settings and create the site collection.

28. When the site collection is created, click *OK*.

29. Close Internet Explorer.

Exercise 11.3	Configure Basic Authentication
Overview	In the following exercise, you will create an application that uses Basic authentication. You will then create a site collection for the Web application.
Completion time	15 minutes

1. Open *Central Administration*.

2. Click *Application Management*.

3. In the Web Applications section, click *Manage Web Applications*. The Web Applications Management page displays.

4. On the Ribbon, click *New*.

5. Change the port to *2002*.

6. While the *Create new application pool* is selected, click the *Configuration* drop-down arrow and select the *contoso\SPAdminXX* account.

7. Click *OK*.

8. When the application is created, click *OK*.

9. Click *http://StudentXX:2002*.

10. On the Ribbon, click Authentication Providers. The Authentication Providers page displays.

11. Click *Default*. The Edit Authentication page displays.

12. In the IIS Authentication Settings section, select the *Basic Authentication* check box.

Question 1	Why is Basic authentication insecure?

Question 2	How would you secure Basic authentication?

13. At the bottom of the page, click *Save*.

14. Close the Authentication Providers page.

15. Click *Application Management*.

16. In the *Site Collections*, section, click *Create site collections*.

17. If necessary, change the Web application to *http://StudentXX:2002*. If you need to change the Web application, click the current web application and then click *Change Web Application*. Click *SharePoint – 2002*.

18. In the *Title* text box, type *Basic*.

19. In the *Primary Site Collection Administrators* text box, type *contoso\StudentXX*.

20. In the *Secondary Site Collection Administrators* text box, type *contoso\SPAdminXX*.

21. Click *OK* to accept your settings and create the site collection.

22. When the site collection is created, click *OK*.

23. Launch Internet Explorer and go to *http://StudentXX:2002*.

24. Close Internet Explorer.

Exercise 11.4	Configure and Manage Claims-Based Authentication
Overview	In the following exercise, you will create an application that uses Claims-Based authentication. You will then create a site collection for the Web application.
Completion time	10 minutes

1. Open *Central Administration*.

2. Click *Application Management*. The Application Management page displays.

3. In the Web Applications section, click *Manage Web Applications*.

4. On the Ribbon, click *New*. The Create New Web Application page displays.

5. In the *Authentication* section, select *Claims Based Authentication*.

6. Change the port to *2003*.

7. While the *Create new application pool* is selected, select the *contoso\SPAdminXX* account.

8. In the *Claims Authentication Types* section, make sure the *Enable Windows Authentication* and *Integrated Windows authentication* is selected. In addition, make sure *NTLM* is selected.

9. At the bottom of the page, click *OK*.

10. When the application is created, click *OK*.

11. Click *Application Management*.

12. Click *Create site collections*.

13. If necessary, change the Web application to *http://StudentXX:2003*. (To change the Web application, click the current Web application, click *Change Web Application*, and then click *SharePoint – 2003*).

14. In the *Title* text box, type *Basic*.

15. In the *Primary Site Collection Administrators* text box, type *contoso\StudentXX*.

16. For the *Secondary Site Collection Administrators* text box, type *contoso\SPAdminXX*.

17. Click *OK* to accept your changes and create the site collection.

18. When the site collection is created, click *OK*.

19. Launch Internet Explorer and go to *http://StudentXX:2003*.

20. Close Internet Explorer.

LAB 12
BACKING UP AND RESTORING A SHAREPOINT 2010 ENVIRONMENT

THIS LAB CONTAINS THE FOLLOWING EXERCISES AND ACTIVITIES:

Exercise 12.1   Back Up SharePoint 2010 with Central Administration

Exercise 12.2   Restore SharePoint 2010 with Central Administration

Exercise 12.3   Perform a SharePoint 2010 Backup using SQL Tools

Exercise 12.4   Restore a Database Using SQL Tools

Exercise 12.5   Recover Data from an Unattached Content Database

BEFORE YOU BEGIN

The lab environment consists of student workstations connected to a local area network, along with a server that functions as the domain controller for a domain called contoso.com. The computers required for this lab are listed in Table 12-1.

Table 12-1
Computers required for Lab 12

Computer	Operating System	Computer Name
Instructor Server	Windows Server 2008 R2	RWDC01
Student Server	Windows Server 2008 R2	Studentxx, where xx is your Student number.

> **NOTE**
>
> *In a classroom lab or virtual lab environment, there will be one classroom server and the students will have workstations named using consecutive numbers in place of the XX variable.*

In addition to the computers, you will also need the software listed in Table 12-2 in order to complete Lab 12.

Table 12-2
Software required for Lab 12

Software	Location
Lab 12 student worksheet	Lab12_worksheet.rtf (provided by instructor)

Working with Lab Worksheets

Each lab in this manual requires that you answer questions, shoot screen shots, and perform other activities that you will document in a worksheet named for the lab (such as Lab12_worksheet.rtf). Your instructor will provide you with access to the worksheets. It is recommended that you use a USB flash drive to store your worksheets, so you can submit them to your instructor for review. As you perform the exercises in each lab, open the appropriate worksheet file using WordPad, fill in the required information, and save the file to your flash drive.

SCENARIO

Now that you have put a lot of work into establishing your SharePoint environment, you are ready to make sure that you can recover SharePoint data at any time. Therefore, you need to back up your SharePoint environment and perform a restore to verify that the backups are working.

After completing this lab, you will be able to:

- Back up a SharePoint farm

- Restore SharePoint components

- Back up and restore a SQL database

- Recover data from an unattached content database

Estimated lab time: 75 minutes

Exercise 12.1	Back Up SharePoint 2010 with Central Administration
Overview	In the following exercise, you will use Central Administration to back up the entire SharePoint farm.
Completion time	30 minutes

1. On your student server, log in as *contoso\Studentxx* (*xx* represents your student number) and use *Pa$$w0rd* as the password.

2. Click *Start* and then click *Computer*. Double-click *Local Disk (C:)*.

3. Create a new folder named *Backup*.

4. Close the *Local Disk (C:)* folder.

5. Open *Central Administration*.

6. Click *Backup and Restore*. The Backup and Restore page displays.

7. Click *Configure backup settings*.

Question 1	What is the default number of backup threads?

Question 2	What is the default number of restore threads?

8. Change the number of default backup threads and restore threads to *5*.

9. In the *Backup File Location* section, in the *Backup location* text box, type *C:\Backup*.

10. Click *OK* to accept your settings and return to the Backup and Restore page.

11. In the *Farm Backup and Restore* section, click *Perform a Backup*. The Perform a Backup – Step 1 of 2: Select Component to Backup page displays.

12. Select the *Farm* check box.

13. Click *Next*. The Perform a Backup – Step 2 of 2: Select Backup Options displays.

14. Click *Start Backup*. The Backup and Restore Job Status page displays.

15. After 15 seconds, click *Refresh*. The screen will refresh from time to time. However, you can click *Refresh* at any time.

16. Close Internet Explorer.

Exercise 12.2	Restore SharePoint 2010 with Central Administration
Overview	In the following exercise, you will use Central Administration to restore a SharePoint component from a farm backup.
Completion time	10 minutes

1. Open *Central Administration*.

2. Click *Backup and Restore*.

3. In the Farm Backup and Restore section, click *Restore from a backup*. The Restore from Backup - Step 1 of 3: Select Backup to Restore page displays.

4. Select the backup job that you just performed and then click *Next*. A list of all the components present in the backup files is displayed.

5. Expand *Microsoft SharePoint Foundation Web Application* and then expand *SharePoint – 2000*. Select the content database for SharePoint – 2000. Click *Next*.

6. In the *Restore Options* section, select *Same Configuration*.

7. When you are warned that all selected components will be overwritten, click *OK*.

8. Click *Start Restore*. The Backup and Restore Job Status page displays the progress of the restore operation.

9. After about a minute, click the *View History* option. Verify that the restore completed.

10. Close *Central Administration*.

Exercise 12.3	Perform a Database Backup with SQL Tools
Overview	In the following exercise, you will back up a database using SQL Server Management Studio.
Completion time	10 minutes

1. Click *Start* > *All Programs* > *SQL Server 2008 R2* > *SQL Server Management Studio*.

2. When the Connect to Server dialog box displays, make sure the *Server name* text box displays the *StudentXX* server and then click *Connect*.

3. In Object Explorer, expand *Databases*.

4. Right-click *WSS_Content_SSL*, choose *Tasks*, and then choose *Back Up*. The Backup Database page displays.

5. In the *Source* section, make sure that the Backup type is set to *Full*.

6. In the *Destination* section, click the backup file that is listed and then click *Remove*.

7. Click *Add*.

8. Click the . . . button.

9. In the the *File name* text box, type *C:\Backup\SSL.BAK* and then click *OK*.

10. Click *OK* to close the Select Backup Destination.

11. In the Backup Database dialog box, click *OK*.

12. When the backup is successful, click *OK*.

13. Close Microsoft SQL Server Management Studio.

Exercise 12.4	Restore a Database using SQL Tools
Overview	In the following exercise, you will restore a SQL database using SQL Server Management Studio.
Completion time	10 minutes

1. Click *Start* > *All Programs* > *SQL Server 2008 R2* > *SQL Server Management Studio*.

2. When the Connect to Server dialog box displays, make sure the *Server name* text box displays the *StudentXX* server and then click *Connect*.

3. In Object Explorer, expand *Databases*.

4. Right-click *WSS_Content_SSL* and select *Delete*.

5. When the Delete Object dialog box displays, select *Close existing connections* and then click *OK*.

6.   Right-click **Databases** and select **Restore Database**.

7.   Select **From device**. The Restore database displays.

8.   Click the . . . button. The Specify Database dialog box displays.

9.   Click **Add**.

10.   Navigate to the **C:\Backup\SSL.BAK** and click **OK**.

11.   Click **OK** to accept your settings and close the Specify Backup dialog box.

12.   Select the **Restore** check box for the **WSS_Content_SSL** database.

13.   Click the **To database** down arrow and select **WSS_Content_SSL**.

14.   Click the **Options** page.

15.   Select **Overwrite the existing database (WITH REPLACE)**.

16.   Click **OK**.

17.   When the restore is successful, click **OK**.

18.   Close SQL Server Management Studio.

Exercise 12.5	Recover Data from an Unattached Content Database
Overview	In the following exercise, you will backup and restore a SQL database. You will then export a library from the unattached database.
Completion time	15 minutes

1.   Click **Start > All Programs > SQL Server 2008 R2 > SQL Server Management Studio**.

2.   When the Connect to Server dialog box displays, make sure the **Server name** text box displays the **StudentXX** server and then click **Connect**.

3.   In Object Explorer, expand **Databases**.

4.   Right-click the **WSS_Content** database and select **Back Up**.

5.   In the **Destination** section, with the BAK file highlighted, click **Remove**.

6.   Click **Add**. The Select Destination dialog box opens.

7.   Click the . . . button.

8.   In the **File name** text box, type **c:\Backup\Content.BAK** and then click **OK**.

9.   Click *OK*.

10. When the backup is complete, click *OK*.

11. Right-click *Databases* and choose *Restore Database*.

12. Click *From device* and then click the . . . button. The Specify Backup dialog box displays.

13. Click *Add*.

14. Browse to and select *C:\Backup\Content.bak*. Click *OK* to accept your settings and close the Locate Backup File dialog box.

15. Click *OK* to accept your settings and close the Specify Backup dialog box.

16. In the To database dialog box, type *WSSContentBak*.

17. Select the *Restore* check box.

18. Click *OK*.

19. When the Restore is complete, click *OK*.

20. Close *Microsoft SQL Server Management Studio*.

21. Open *Central Administration*.

22. Click *Backup and Restore*. The Backup and Restore page displays.

23. In the Granular Backup section, click *Recover data from an unattached content database*. The Unattached Content Database Data Recovery page displays.

24. In the *Database Name* text box, type *wsscontentbak*.

25. Make sure the Browse content (default) option is selected and then click *Next*. The Browse content page opens.

26. Click the *Site* down arrow, click *No selection*, and then click *Change Site*.

27. With the /URL selected, click *OK*.

28. Click the *List* drop-down arrow, click *No Selection* and then click *Change List*. Click *Documents* and then click *OK*.

29. Click *Export site or list*.

30. For the *Filename* text box, click *C:\Backup\DocumentList.bak*.

31. Click *Start Export*.

32. When the export is completed, close Internet Explorer.

APPENDIX:
LAB SETUP GUIDE

GETTING STARTED

The Microsoft SharePoint 2010 Configuration title of the Microsoft Official Academic Course (MOAC) series includes two books: a textbook and a lab manual. The exercises in the lab manual are designed either for a virtual machine environment or for classroom use under the supervision of an instructor or lab aide. In an academic setting, the computer lab might be used by a variety of classes each day, so you must plan your setup procedure accordingly. For example, consider automating the classroom setup procedure and using removable hard disks in the classroom. You can use the automated setup procedure to rapidly configure the classroom environment, and remove the fixed disks after teaching this class each day.

LAB CONFIGURATION

This course should be taught in a lab containing networked computers where students can develop their skills through hands-on experience with Microsoft Windows Server 2008 R2 and SharePoint 2010. The exercises in the lab manual require the computers to be installed and configured in a specific manner. Failure to adhere to the setup instructions in this document can produce unanticipated results when the students perform the exercises.

The lab configuration consists of an instructor server and student servers running Microsoft Windows Server 2008 R2 Enterprise and student computers running a number of workstations.

The Instructor server will act as a domain controller and Microsoft Exchange server. It will also act as a SharePoint server, which will be used for demonstrations in the classroom and for students to perform the exercises in Lab 1. For self-contained virtual environment, each student will need two servers: A Windows Server 2008 R2/SharePoint server and a domain controller/Microsoft Exchange Server.

The lab uses the following information for the AD DS and server configuration:

- Active Directory Domain Services domain name: contoso.com
- Computer name: RWDC01
- Fully qualified domain name (FQDN): rwdc01.contoso.com

This document includes a setup procedure that configures the server to provide all the infrastructure services required throughout the course. Once you have completed the initial setup, no further modifications to the lab server should be necessary.

The workstations in the lab are named Student*xx*, where *xx* is a unique student number assigned to each computer. Each workstation will be a member of the contoso.com domain throughout most of the exercises, and also have a local administrative account called Student.

NOTE	*For the purposes of this lab, all server and workstation passwords, for user accounts and other purposes, will be set to Pa$$w0rd. This password is obviously a weak password in a real-world situation, and instructors should remind students of this at the outset.*

Some lab exercises have dependencies on previous exercises, as noted in the lab manual and the instructor notes for each exercise. Students should perform the lab exercises in order and students might have to complete any exercises they have missed due to absence before proceeding to the next lab.

Instructor Server Requirements

The instructor computer running Windows Server 2008 R2 in the classroom requires the following hardware and software:

Hardware Requirements

- Minimum Processor: Dual-Core x64 processor
- Minimum RAM: 4 GB recommended
- Minimum Disk Space: 160 GB
- DVD drive
- Network interface adapter
- Minimum: Super VGA (1024x768) display
- Keyboard
- Mouse

Software Requirements

All of the software listed below is required for this course:

- **Microsoft Windows Server 2008 R2 Enterprise with SP1.** The evaluation edition can be downloaded at http://www.microsoft.com/windowsserver2008/en/us/trial-software.aspx.
- **2007 Office System Converter.** The Microsoft Filter Pack (FilterPackx64.exe) can be downloaded at http://www.microsoft.com/download/en/details.aspx?id=20109.
- **Windows Installer 4.5 Redistributable** (required for SQL Server 2008 R2 installation) can be downloaded at http://www.microsoft.com/download/en/details.aspx?displaylang=en&id=8483.
- **Microsoft Exchange Server 2010 with SP1.** The evaluation edition can be downloaded at http://technet.microsoft.com/en-us/evalcenter/dd185495.

- **SQL Server 2008 R2 Enterprise Edition.** The evaluation edition can be downloaded at http://www.microsoft.com/sqlserver/en/us/get-sql-server/try-it.aspx.

- **Microsoft SharePoint 2010 for Enterprise Client Access License.** The evaluation version can be downloaded at http://www.microsoft.com/download/en/details.aspx?displaylang=en&id=16631.

- **Windows Identity Foundation (KB974405) Windows6.1-KB974405-x64.msu** can be downloaded at http://www.microsoft.com/download/en/details.aspx?displaylang=en&id=17331.

- **Microsoft Sync Framework Runtime v1.0 (x64) SyncSetup_en.x64.zip** can be downloaded at http://www.microsoft.com/download/en/details.aspx?id=15391.

- **Microsoft Chart Controls for Microsoft .NET Framework 3.5 MSChart.exe** can be downloaded at http://www.microsoft.com/download/en/details.aspx?displaylang=en&id=14422.

- **Microsoft Filter Pack 2.0 FilterPack64bit.exe** can be downloaded at http://www.microsoft.com/download/en/details.aspx?id=17062.

- **Microsoft SQL Server 2008 Analysis Services ADOMD.NET SQLSERVER2008_ASADOMD10.msi** can be downloaded at http://go.microsoft.com/fwlink/?LinkId=130651.

- **Microsoft Server Speech Platform Runtime (x64) Platform\x64\SpeechPlatformRuntime.msi** can be downloaded at http://www.microsoft.com/download/en/details.aspx?displaylang=en&id=16789.

- **Microsoft Server Speech Recognition Language - TELE(en-US) SR\MSSpeech_SR_en-US_TELE.msi** can be downloaded at http://www.microsoft.com/download/en/details.aspx?amp;displaylang=en&id=24139.

- **SQL 2008 R2 Reporting Services SharePoint 2010 Add-in 1033\x64\rsSharePoint.msi** can be downloaded at http://www.microsoft.com/download/en/details.aspx?displaylang=en&id=622

- **Hotfix for WCF: SharePoint Shared Services Roll-up (Windows6.1-KB976462-v2-x64.msu)** can be downloaded at https://connect.microsoft.com/VisualStudio/Downloads/DownloadDetails.aspx?DownloadID=23806

- **SharePoint 2010 SP1 officeserver2010sp1-kb2460045-x64-fullfile-en-us.exe** can be downloaded at http://www.microsoft.com/download/en/details.aspx?id=26623

- Description of the **SharePoint Server 2010 cumulative update refresh package** (SharePoint server-package): August 30, 2011 office2010kb2553048fullfilex64glb can be downloaded at http://support.microsoft.com/kb/2553048

- **Microsoft Office 2010 Professional (x17-75058.exe)** is available as an evaluation download at http://office.microsoft.com/en-us/try/try-office-2010-FX101868838.aspx.

- **Windows Server 2008 R2 Multilingual User Interface Language Packs – French (Windows6.1-KB2483139-x64-fr-FR.exe)** can be downloaded at http://www.microsoft.com/download/en/details.aspx?displaylang=en&id=1246. Be sure to select French before downloading.

- **2010 Server Language Packs for SharePoint Server 2010, Project Server 2010, Search Server 2010, and Office Web Apps 2010 – French (ServerLanguagePack.exe)** can be downloaded at http://www.microsoft.com/download/en/details.aspx?displaylang=en&id=3411. Be sure to change the language to French before downloading.

- **WSS_Content_30.bak** can be downloaded from the Wiley companion site.

- **SharePointLogger.wsp** and **PrintList.wsp** can be downloaded at http://sandbox.codeplex.com/releases/view/34976.

Student Server Requirements

Each workstation requires the following hardware and software:

Hardware Requirements

- Minimum Processor: Dual-Core ×64 processor
- Minimum RAM: 4 GB recommended
- Minimum Disk Space: 160 GB
- DVD drive
- Network interface adapter
- Minimum: Super VGA (1024 × 768) display
- Keyboard
- Mouse

Software Requirements

All of the software listed below is required for the course.

- **Microsoft Windows Server 2008 R2 Enterprise with SP1 – evaluation edition** can be downloaded at http://www.microsoft.com/windowsserver2008/en/us/trial-software.aspx.
- **Microsoft SQL Server 2008 R2 RTM - Express with Management Tools, SQLEXPRWT_x64_ENU.exe** can be downloaded at http://www.microsoft.com/download/en/details.aspx?id=23650.
- **2007 Office System Converter: Microsoft Filter Pack (FilterPackx64.exe)** can be downloaded at http://www.microsoft.com/download/en/details.aspx?id=20109.
- **Windows Installer 4.5 Redistributable, Windows6.0-KB942288-v2-x64.msu** (required for SQL Server 2008 R2 installation) can be downloaded at http://www.microsoft.com/download/en/details.aspx?displaylang=en&id=8483.
- **Microsoft SharePoint 2010 for Enterprise Client Access License evaluation** can be downloaded at http://www.microsoft.com/download/en/details.aspx?displaylang=en&id=16631.
- **Windows Identity Foundation (KB974405) Windows6.1-KB974405-x64.msu** can be downloaded at http://www.microsoft.com/download/en/details.aspx?displaylang=en&id=17331.
- **Microsoft Sync Framework Runtime v1.0 (x64) SyncSetup_en.x64.zip** can be downloaded at http://www.microsoft.com/download/en/details.aspx?id=15391.
- **Microsoft Chart Controls for Microsoft .NET Framework 3.5 MSChart.exe** can be downloaded at http://www.microsoft.com/download/en/details.aspx?displaylang=en&id=14422.
- **Microsoft Filter Pack 2.0 FilterPack64bit.exe** can be downloaded at http://www.microsoft.com/download/en/details.aspx?id=17062.
- **Microsoft SQL Server 2008 Analysis Services ADOMD.NET SQLSERVER2008_ASADOMD10.msi** can be downloaded at http://go.microsoft.com/fwlink/?LinkId=130651.
- **Microsoft Server Speech Platform Runtime (x64) Platform\x64\SpeechPlatformRuntime.msi** can be downloaded at http://www.microsoft.com/download/en/details.aspx?displaylang=en&id=16789.

- **Microsoft Server Speech Recognition Language - TELE(en-US) SR\MSSpeech_SR_en-US_TELE.msi** can be downloaded at http://www.microsoft.com/download/en/details.aspx?amp;displaylang=en&id=24139.

- **SQL 2008 R2 Reporting Services SharePoint 2010 Add-in 1033\x64\rsSharePoint.msi** can be downloaded at http://www.microsoft.com/download/en/details.aspx?displaylang=en&id=622

- **Hotfix for WCF: SharePoint Shared Services Roll-up (Windows6.1-KB976462-v2-x64.msu)** can be downloaded at https://connect.microsoft.com/VisualStudio/Downloads/DownloadDetails.aspx?DownloadID=23806

- **SharePoint 2010 SP1 officeserver2010sp1-kb2460045-x64-fullfile-en-us.exe** can be downloaded at http://www.microsoft.com/download/en/details.aspx?id=26623

- Description of the **SharePoint Server 2010 cumulative update refresh package** (SharePoint server-package): August 30, 2011 office2010kb2553048fullfilex64glb can be downloaded at http://support.microsoft.com/kb/2553048

- **Microsoft Office 2010 Professional (x17-75058.exe)** can be downloaded at http://office.microsoft.com/en-us/try/try-office-2010-FX101868838.aspx.

- **ULS Viewer** can be downloaded at http://archive.msdn.microsoft.com/ULSViewer.

- **Windows Server 2008 R2 Multilingual User Interface Language Packs – French (Windows6.1-KB2483139-x64-fr-FR.exe)** can be downloaded at http://www.microsoft.com/download/en/details.aspx?displaylang=en&id=1246. Be sure to select French before downloading.

- **2010 Server Language Packs for SharePoint Server 2010, Project Server 2010, Search Server 2010, and Office Web Apps 2010 – French (ServerLanguagePack.exe)** can be downloaded at http://www.microsoft.com/download/en/details.aspx?displaylang=en&id=3411. Be sure to change the language to French before downloading.

- **WSS_Content_30.bak** can be downloaded from the Wiley companion site.

- **SharePointLogger.wsp** and **PrintList.wsp** can be downloaded at http://sandbox.codeplex.com/releases/view/34976.

INSTRUCTOR SERVER SETUP INSTRUCTIONS

Before you begin, perform the following:

- Read this entire document.
- Make sure you have the Instructor installation disks for Microsoft Windows Server 2008 R2.

Installing the Instructor Server	
Overview	Use the following setup procedure to install Windows Server 2008 R2 on RWDC01. This procedure assumes that you are performing a clean installation of the Windows Server 2008 R2 Enterprise evaluation edition and that if you have downloaded an image file, you have already burned it to a DVD-ROM disk. For a virtual environment, you must place copies of the installation ISOs on their hard drives so that you can mount the ISO image as the DVD disk.
Completion time	20 minutes

> **WARNING**
>
> *By performing the following setup instructions, your computer's hard disks will be repartitioned and reformatted. You will lose all existing data on these systems.*

1. Turn on the computer and insert the *Windows Server 2008 R2 installation DVD* into the drive. If you are using a virtual environment, you will have to mount the ISO image.

2. Press any key, if necessary, to boot from the DVD-ROM disk. The Setup program loads and the Install Windows window displays. If you are using a virtual environment, boot from the ISO image.

3. Modify the *Language to install*, *Time and currency format*, and *Keyboard or input method* settings, if necessary, and then click *Next*.

4. Click *Install Now*. The Select the operating system you want to install page displays.

5. Select *Windows Server 2008 R2 Enterprise (Full Installation)* and click *Next*. The Please read the license terms page displays.

6. Select the *I accept the license terms* check box and click *Next*. The Which type of installation do you want? page displays.

7. Click *Custom (advanced)*. The Where do you want to install Windows? page displays.

> **NOTE**
>
> *If there are existing partitions on the computer's hard disk, select each one in turn and delete it before proceeding.*

8. Select *Disk 0 Unallocated Space* and then click *Next*. The Installing Windows page displays, indicating the progress of the Setup program as it installs the operating system. After the installation completes and the computer restarts, a message displays stating that the user's password must be changed before logging on the first time.

9. Click *OK*. A Windows logon screen displays.

10. In the *New password* and *Confirm Password* text boxes, type *Pa$$w0rd* and click the right-arrow button. A message displays, stating that Your password has been changed.

11. Click *OK*. The logon process completes and the Initial Configuration Tasks window displays.

Once the installation process is finished, you must proceed to perform the following tasks to configure the server and install the necessary roles to support the student workstations.

Completing Initial Server Configuration Tasks

Perform the following configuration tasks before you install Active Directory Domain Services or any other roles on the server.

Configuring Date and Time Settings

Overview	To configure time and date settings, perform the following steps.
Completion time	5 minutes

1. In the Initial Configuration Tasks window, click *Set time zone*. The Date and Time dialog box displays.

2. If the time and/or date shown in the dialog box are not correct, click *Change date and time* and, in the Date and Time Settings dialog box, set the correct date and time and then click *OK*.

3. If the time zone is not correct for your location, click *Change time zone* and, in the Time Zone Settings dialog box, set the correct time zone and then click *OK*.

Configuring TCP/IP Settings

Overview	To configure TCP/IP settings, perform the following steps.
Completion time	5 minutes

1. In the Initial Configuration Tasks window, click *Configure networking*. The Network Connections window displays.

2. Right-click the *Local Area Connection* icon and, from the context menu, select *Properties*. The Local Area Connection Properties sheet displays.

3. Select *Internet Protocol Version 4 (TCP/IPv4)* and click *Properties*. The Internet Protocol Version 4 (TCP/IPv4) Properties sheet displays.

4. Select the *Use the following IP address* option and configure the following settings:

    *   IP address: *10.10.0.31*
    *   Subnet mask: *255.255.255.0*
    *   Default gateway: Leave blank
    *   Preferred DNS server: *10.10.0.31*
    *   Alternate DNS server: Leave blank

5. Click *OK* to accept your settings and close the Internet Protocol Version 4 (TCP/IPv4) Properties sheet.

6. Click *Close* to close the Local Area Connection Properties sheet.

7. Close the Network Connections window.

Naming the Server

Overview	To name the server, perform the following steps.
Completion time	5 minutes

1. In the Initial Configuration Tasks window, click *Provide computer name and domain*. The System Properties sheet displays.

2. Click *Change*. The Computer Name/Domain Changes dialog box displays.

3. In the *Computer name* text box, type *RWDC01* and then click *OK*.

4. A Computer Name/Domain Changes message box displays, stating that you must restart the computer.

5. Click *OK*.

6. Click *Close* to close the System Properties dialog box. A Microsoft Windows message box displays, instructing you again to restart the computer.

7. Click *Restart Now*. The system restarts.

Installing Server Roles

After configuring the Windows server, you can install the server roles needed to support the student workstation, as described in the following sections.

Installing Active Directory Domain Services

Overview	To install Active Directory Domain Services, perform the following steps.
Completion time	15 minutes

1. Log on to the server using the *Administrator* account and the *Pa$$w0rd* password. The Initial Configuration Tasks window displays.

2. Under Customize This Server, click *Add roles*. The Add Roles Wizard displays.

3. Click *Next* to advance past the Before You Begin page. The Select Server Roles page displays.

4. Select the *Active Directory Domain Services* check box. The Add features required for Active Directory Domain Services? dialog box displays.

5. Click *Add Required Features* and then click *Next*. The Introduction to Active Directory Domain Services page displays.

6. Click *Next*. The Confirm Installation Selections page displays.

7. Click *Install*. The Installation Results page displays.

8. Click *Close this wizard and launch the Active Directory Domain Services Installation Wizard (dcpromo.exe)*. The Active Directory Domain Services Installation Wizard displays.

9. Click *Next* to advance past the Welcome page. The Operating System Compatibility page displays.

10. Click *Next*. The Choose a Deployment Configuration page displays.

11. Select the *Create a new domain in a new forest* option and click *Next*. The Name the Forest Root Domain page displays.

12. In the FWDN of the forest root domain text box, type *contoso.com* and click *Next*. The Set Forest Functional Level page displays.

13. In the Forest functional level drop-down list, select *Windows Server 2008 R2* and click *Next*. The Additional Domain Controller options page displays.

14. Click *Next*. An Active Directory Domain Services Installation Wizard message box displays.

15. Click *Yes*. The Location for Database, Log Files, and SYSVOL page displays.

16. Click *Next*. The Directory Services Restore Mode Administrator Password page displays.

17. In the Password and Confirm Password text boxes, type *Pa$$w0rd* and then click *Next*. The Summary page displays.

18. Click *Next*. The wizard installs Active Directory Domain Services. The Completing the Active Directory Domain Services Installation Wizard page displays.

19. Click *Finish* and then click *Restart Now*. The computer restarts.

Installing Exchange Server

Overview	The student workstations in the lab do not require access to the Internet, as long as the software the students need to install as they perform the exercises is available on the lab server. To prepare the server, perform the following steps.
Completion time	30 minutes

1. Log on to the server using the *Administrator* account and the *Pa$$w0rd* password.

2. Using Active Directory Users and Computers, create a user account named *Svc-Exchange* in the Users container and assign the account the *Pa$$w0rd* password.

3. Configure the password to never expire. Add this user account to the *Enterprise Admins*, *Domain Admins*, and *Schema Admins* groups.

4. Using the Server Manager console, add *Svc-Exchange* to the local *Administrators* group.

5. Open an elevated command prompt and navigate to the directory that contains the Exchange Server 2010 setup files.

6. In the elevated command prompt, execute the following command:

    ```
    Setup /PrepareSchema
    ```

7. In the elevated command prompt, execute the following command

    ```
    Setup /PrepareAD /OrganizationName:contoso.com
    ```

8. Add the *Svc-Exchange* user account to the Organization Management group in the Microsoft Exchange Security Groups container.

9. From the elevated command prompt, execute the following command:

    ```
    Setup /PrepareAllDomains
    ```

10. Install the Office System Converter: Microsoft Filter Pack x64 by double-clicking installation file. Click *Next* and accept the license terms.

11. Open an elevated PowerShell session and execute the following command:

    ```
    Import-Module ServerManager
    ```

12. In the elevated PowerShell session, execute the following command:

    ```
    Add-WindowsFeature NET-Framework,RSAT-ADDS,Web-
    Server,Web-Basic-Auth,Web-Windows-Auth,Web-Metabase,Web-
    Net-Ext,Web-Lgcy-Mgmt-Console,WAS-Process-Model,RSAT-Web-
    Server,Web-ISAPI-Ext,Web-Digest-Auth,Web-Dyn-
    Compression,NET-HTTP-Activation,RPCOver-HTTP-Proxy
    ```

13. Restart the server.

14. Log on using the *contoso\Administrator* account.

15. Open an elevated PowerShell session and execute the following command:

    ```
    Import-Module ServerManager
    ```

16. In the elevated PowerShell session, execute the following command:

    ```
    Set-Service -Name NetTcpPortSharing -StartupType Automatic
    ```

17. Log out of the computer.

18. Log on with the *Contoso\Svc-Exchange* account.

19. Use Windows Explorer to navigate to the location of the Exchange installation files.

20. Run *Setup.exe*. When prompted, click *Yes* at the User Account Control dialog box.

21. On the splash screen, click on *Step 3: Choose Exchange Language* Option. Click the *Install Only Languages From The DVD* option.

22. Click *Step 4: Install Microsoft Exchange*.

23. On the Introduction page, click *Next*.

24. On the License Agreement Page, click *I Accept The Terms In The License Agreement* and then click *Next*.

25. On the Error Reporting page, ensure that *No* is selected and then click *Next*.

26. On the Exchange Server 2010 Setup page, ensure that *Typical Exchange Server Installation* is selected and then click *Next*.

27. On the Client Settings page, select *No* when asked whether you have client computers running Outlook 2003 or Entourage and then click *Next*.

28. On the Configure Client Access Server External Domain page, ensure that *The Client Access Server Role Will Be Internet Facing* option is not selected and then click *Next*.

29. On the Customer Experience Improvement Program page, select *I Don't Wish To Join The Program At This Time* and then click *Next*.

30. The readiness checks will now run. Verify that all readiness checks complete successfully and then click *Install*.

31. When setup completes, verify that all stages of the setup are marked as Completed. Click *View Setup Log* to view the Exchange setup log in Notepad. Review the contents of this log by clicking *View Setup* and then close the log. Click *Finish*.

32. On the Exchange Server Setup splash screen, click *Close*. At the warning that informs you about critical updates to Exchange Server, click *Yes*.

33. Exchange Management Console will have automatically opened at this point. Close this console.

Preparing the Server File System

Overview	The student workstations in the lab do not require access to the Internet, as long as the software the students need to install as they perform the exercises is available on the lab server. To prepare the server, perform the following steps.
Completion time	30 minutes

1.   Log on to the server using the *Administrator* account and the *Pa$$w0rd* password. The Initial Configuration Tasks window displays.

2.   On the RWDC01 server, open Windows Explorer and create a new folder on the C:\ directory called *Downloads*.

3.   Right-click the *Downloads* folder and select *Properties*.

4.   Select the *Sharing* tab, click *Advanced Sharing* and then select *Share this folder*.

5.   Click *OK* to accept your settings and close the Advanced Sharing dialog box.

6.   Click *OK* to close Downloads Properties.

7.   Download all of the software products previously listed in the Software Requirements sections (instructor and student) of this document and then place them into the Downloads folder.

8.   In the Downloads folder, create a subfolder called *SharePoint2010*.

9.   Open a command prompt.

10.   Within the command prompt window, change to the *C:\Downloads* folder.

11.   Execute the following command:

```
Sharepointserver.exe /extract:C:\Downloads\SharePoint2010
```

Installing SQL Server 2008 R2

Overview	To install SQL Server 2008 R2, perform the following steps.
Completion time	20 minutes

1.   Log on to the server using the *Administrator* account and the *Pa$$w0rd* password. The Initial Configuration Tasks window displays.

2.   Using Active Directory Users and Computers, create a user account named *Svc-SQL* in the Users container and assign the account the password *Pa$$w0rd*.

3.   Log in as *contoso\Svc-SQL*.

4.   Open the SQL Server 2008 R2 installation folder and double-click *setup.exe*. If a User Account Control dialog box displays, click *Yes*.

5. When the SQL Server Installation Center displays, click the *Installation* link on the left side of the window.

6. Click *New installation or add features to an existing installation*.

7. When the Setup Support rules have passed, click *OK*.

8. When you're prompted to provide the product key, leave the default setting and click *Next*.

9. When you're prompted for the License Terms, select *I accept the license terms* and then click *Next*.

10. When you're prompted to install the Setup Support Files, click *Install*.

11. After the Setup Support Rules have passed again, click *Next*.

12. Select *SQL Server Feature Installation* and then click *Next*.

13. On the Feature Selection page, select *Database Engine Services, Reporting Services, Management Tools – Complete* and then click *Next*.

14. When the Installation Rules pass, click *Next*.

15. Leave the Default instance selected and then click *Next*.

16. On the Disk Space Requirements page, click *Next*.

17. On the Server Configuration page, click the *Use the same account for all SQL Server services* button. Specify the account name of *contoso\svc-sql* and use the *Pa$$w0rd* password.

18. Click *OK* and then click *Next*.

19. When the Database Engine Configuration page displays, leave *Windows authentication mode* selected and click the *Add current User* button. Click *Next*.

20. On the Reporting Services Configuration page, click the *Install the SharePoint integrated mode default configuration* and then click *Next*.

21. On the Error Reporting page displays, click *Next*.

22. When the Installation Configuration Rules pass, click *Next*.

23. When the Ready to Install page displays, click *Install*.

24. When the installation is complete, click *Close*.

25. Close the SQL Server Installation window.

Installing SharePoint Prerequisites

Overview	To install SharePoint prerequisites, perform the following steps.
Completion time	20 minutes

1.   Log on to the server as the *contoso\SVC-SQL* account.

2.   Go to the installation disk or folder that holds the SharePoint 2010 installation files and then double-click the SharePoint executable.

3.   If the Open File – Security Warning dialog box displays, prompting you to confirm that you want to run the file, click *Yes*.

4.   When the Microsoft SharePoint 2010 splash screen displays, click *Install software prerequisites*.

> **NOTE**
>
> *Since the prerequisite installer downloads components from the Microsoft Download Center, you must have Internet access on the computer. If not, you will have to install each of the prerequisites manually. The prerequisites are located in the download folder. This includes:*
>
> - *Windows Identity Foundation (KB974405) Windows6.1-KB974405-x64.msu*
> - *Microsoft Sync Framework Runtime v1.0 (x64) SyncSetup_en.x64.zip*
> - *Microsoft Chart Controls for Microsoft .NET Framework 3.5 MSChart.exe*
> - *Microsoft Filter Pack 2.0 FilterPack64bit.exe*
> - *Microsoft SQL Server 2008 Analysis Services ADOMD.NET SQLSERVER2008_ASADOMD10.msi*
> - *Microsoft Server Speech Platform Runtime (x64) Platform\x64\SpeechPlatformRuntime.msi*
> - *Microsoft Server Speech Recognition Language - TELE(en-US) SR\MSSpeech_SR_en-US_TELE.msi*
> - *SQL 2008 R2 Reporting Services SharePoint 2010 Add-in 1033\x64\rsSharePoint.msi*
> - *Hotfix for WCF: SharePoint Shared Services Roll-up (Windows6.1-KB976462-v2-x64.msu)*

5.   When the Microsoft SharePoint 2010 Products Preparation Tool wizard begins, click *Next*.

6.   When the License Agreement displays, select the *I accept the terms of the License Agreement(s)* check box and then click *Next*.

7.   When the prerequisites are installed, click *Finish* and then reboot Windows.

Installing SharePoint Binaries

Overview	To install SharePoint binaries, perform the following steps.
Completion time	15 minutes

1.   Log on to the server as the *contoso\SVC-SQL* account.

2.   Go to the installation disk or folder the holds the SharePoint 2010 installation files. Double-click the SharePoint executable.

3.   When the Microsoft Windows SharePoint 2010 splash screen displays, click the *Install SharePoint Server* option.

4.   When prompted for the *Product Key*, type the key. The evaluation key for SharePoint Server 2010 with Enterprise Client Access License features is *VK7BD-VBKWR-6FHD9-Q3HM9-6PKMX*.

5.   When the License Agreement displays, select *I accept the terms of this License Agreement* and then click *Continue*.

6.   When prompted for the type of installation, click the *Server Farm* button.

7.   Select the *Complete – Install all components* option.

8.   Click *Install Now*.

9.   When the Run Configuration Wizard box displays, make sure the *Run the SharePoint Products Configuration Wizard now* option is selected and then click *Close*.

10.   When the SharePoint Configuration Wizard displays, click *Next*.

11.   When you're warned that some services must be restarted, click *Yes*.

12.   To create a new farm, select the *Create a new server farm* option and then click *Next*.

13.   For the Database server, specify the name of the SQL server and its instance name *rwdc01*.

14.   For the *Username* and *Password* entries, type *contoso\svc-sql* and *Pa$w0rd* and then click *Next*.

15.   The passphrase is used to add servers to a farm. Type *Pa$$w0rd* for the passphrase in both text boxes and click *Next*. The Configure SharePoint Central Administration Web Application page displays.

16.   Select the *Specify port number* option, type *3000* in the text box, and then click *Next*.

17. When the Completing the SharePoint Products Configuration Wizard displays, click *Next*.

18. When the configuration finishes, click *Finish*. The SharePoint Central Administration tool displays.

19. When you are prompted to help improve SharePoint, click*, No, I don't wish to participate* and then click *OK*.

20. If you just completed a Complete Installation and you are prompted to configure your SharePoint farm, click *Start the Wizard*.

21. When prompted for a service account, use the *contoso\svc-sql* account and then click *Next*.

22. After several minutes, you will be prompted to create the top-level Web site. In the *Title* text box, type *Classroom SharePoint*. Leave the *Team Site* template selected and then click *OK*.

23. After the wizard completes, a summary screen displays. Click *Finish*.

24. Launch Internet Explorer and go to *http://rwdc01* to verify that the SharePoint site is accessible.

Installing SharePoint 2010 SP1 and Cumulative Update

Overview	To install SharePoint 2010 SP1 and Cumulative Update, perform the following steps.
Completion time	20 minutes

1. Log on to the server as the *contoso\SVC-SQL* account.

2. Install the SharePoint 2010 SP1 by double-clicking the *officeserver2010sp1-kb2460045-x64-fullfile-en-us.exe* file.

3. If you are prompted to make changes to the system, click *Yes*.

4. When the license agreement displays, click *Click here to accept the Microsoft Software License Terms* and click *Continue*.

5. When you are prompted to reboot the computer, click *Yes*.

6. Log on to the server as the *contoso\Svc-SQL* account.

7. Install the August 2011 cumulative update by opening the CumulativeUpdate folder and then double-clicking the *office2010-kb2553048-fullfile-x64-glb.exe*.

8. If a UAC warning displays, click *Yes*.

9. When the license terms page displays, select *Click here to accept the Microsoft Software License Terms* and then click *Continue*.

10. When the installation is complete, click *OK*.

11. Click *Start > All Programs > Microsoft SharePoint 2010 Products > SharePoint 2010 Products Configuration Wizard*.

12. If a UAC dialog box displays, click *Yes*.

13. When the Welcome to SharePoint Products page displays, click *Next*.

14. When it states that certain services will need to be restarted, click *Yes*.

15. When the Completing the SharePoint Products Configuration Wizard displays, click *Next*.

16. When the configuration is successful, click *Finish*. The Central Administration page displays.

17. Launch Internet Explorer and go to *http://rwdc01* to verify that the SharePoint site is accessible.

Configuring SharePoint 2010

Overview	To configure SharePoint 2010, perform the following steps.
Completion time	5 minutes

1. Click *Start > All Programs > Microsoft SharePoint 2010 Products > SharePoint 2010 Central Administration*.

2. If a UAC dialog box displays, click *Yes*.

3. Click *System Settings*.

4. Click *Configure Outgoing e-mail settings*.

5. In the *Outbound SMTP server* text box, type *rwdc01.contoso.com*.

6. In the *From address* text box and the *Reply-to address* text box, type *SharePoint@contoso.com*.

7. Click *OK*.

Installing Office 2010 Professional

Overview	To install Office 2010 Professional, perform the following steps.
Completion time	20 minutes

1. Double-click the Office 2010 Professional Installation executable.

2. If a UAC prompt displays, click *Yes*.

3. On the Enter your Product key page, type the 25-character key. The evaluation key for Office 2010 Professional is *GR29P-GRYQM-R8YQP-8KDG4-72M4Y*.

4. Click *Continue*.

5. When the software license terms display, select *I accept the terms of this agreement* and then click *Continue*.

6. Click *Install Now*.

7. When Office is installed, click *Close*.

Creating Student Users

Overview	To create student users, perform the following steps.
Completion time	15 minutes

1. Click *Start > Administrative Tools > Active Directory Users and Computers*.

2. Right-click the domain and click *New > Organizational Unit*. Create an organization unit (OU) called *Students*.

3. Right-click the *Students* OU and select *New > User*.

4. Create a user with the following information:

   - First Name *Student1*
   - Full Name: *Student1*
   - User Login Name: *Student1*
   - Password: *Pa$$w0rd*

5. Create additional student accounts for your students.

6. Go to the **Built-in** organizational unit, right-click **Domain Admins**, and then select **Properties**.

7. Click the **Members** tab.

8. Click **Add** button and then add all students to the Domain Admins group.

9. Click **OK** to accept your settings and close the Domain Admins Properties dialog box.

10. Close **Active Directory Users and Computers**.

11. Click **Start** > **All Programs** > **Microsoft Exchange Server 2010** > **Exchange Management Console**.

12. Expand **Microsoft Exchange On-Premises**, expand **Recipient Configuration**, and then click **Mailbox**.

13. Right-click **Mailbox** and then click **New Mailbox**.

14. When the New Mailbox dialog box displays, with the **User Mailbox** selected, click **Next**.

15. Select **Existing Users**.

16. Click **Add**, select the **StudentXX** accounts, and then press the **Enter** key.

17. When you return to the New Mailbox dialog box, click **Next**.

18. When the Mailbox Settings page displays, click **Next**.

19. Click **New**.

20. When the mailboxes are created, close the **Exchange Management Console**.

21. Go to the SharePoint site (**http://rwdc01**) in Internet Explorer.

22. Click **Site Actions** and then select **Site Settings**.

23. In the Users and Permissions section, click **Site collection administrators**.

24. Add the students into the Site Collection Administrators group.

25. Click **OK**.

STUDENT SERVER SETUP INSTRUCTIONS

During the second lab, the students will be installing SQL Server 2008 R2 Express and SharePoint 2010. Therefore, students must have a computer running Windows Server 2008 R2 with SP1. The following setup procedure shows you how to prepare the student servers for the students. This procedure assumes that you are performing a clean installation of the Windows Server 2008 R2 Enterprise evaluation edition and that if you have downloaded an image file, you have already burned it to a DVD-ROM disk or if you are using a virtual computer, you have mounted the image file.

NOTE	*By performing the following setup instructions, your computer's hard disks will be repartitioned and reformatted. You will lose all existing data on these systems.*

Preparing Student Servers

Overview	To prepare the student servers, perform the following steps.
Completion time	20 minutes

1. Turn the computer on and insert the *Windows Server 2008 R2 installation DVD* into the drive. If you are using a virtual environment, you will have to mount the ISO image.

2. Press any key, if necessary, to boot from the DVD-ROM disk. The Setup program loads and the Install Windows window displays. If you are using a virtual environment, boot from the ISO image.

3. Modify the *Language to install*, *Time and currency format*, and *Keyboard or input method* settings, if necessary, and then click *Next*.

4. Click *Install Now*. The Select the operating system you want to install page displays.

5. Select *Windows Server 2008 R2 Enterprise (Full Installation)* and click *Next*. The Please read the license terms page displays.

6. Select the *I accept the license terms* check box and click *Next*. The Which type of installation do you want? page displays.

7. Click *Custom (advanced)*. The Where do you want to install Windows? page displays.

NOTE	*If there are existing partitions on the computer's hard disk, select each one in turn and delete it before proceeding.*

8. Select *Disk 0 Unallocated Space* and then click *Next*. The Installing Windows page displays, indicating the progress of the Setup program as it installs the operating system. After the installation completes and the computer restarts, a message displays stating that the user's password must be changed before logging on the first time.

9. Click *OK*. A Windows logon screen displays.

10. In the *New password* and *Confirm Password* text boxes, type *Pa$$w0rd* and click the right-arrow button. A message displays, stating that Your password has been changed.

11. Click *OK*. The logon process completes and the Initial Configuration Tasks window displays.

Once the installation process is finished, you must proceed to perform the following tasks to configure the server and install the necessary roles to support the student workstations.

Completing Initial Server Configuration Tasks

Perform the following configuration tasks before you install Active Directory Domain Services or any other roles on the server.

Configuring Date and Time Settings	
Overview	To configure time and date settings, perform the following steps.
Completion time	5 minutes

1. In the Initial Configuration Tasks window, click *Set time zone*. The Date and Time dialog box displays.

2. If the time and/or date shown in the dialog box are not correct, click *Change date and time* and, in the Date and Time Settings dialog box, set the correct date and time and then click *OK*.

3. If the time zone is not correct for your location, click *Change time zone* and, in the Time Zone Settings dialog box, set the correct time zone and then click *OK*.

Configuring TCP/IP Settings	
Overview	To configure TCP/IP settings, perform the following steps.
Completion time	5 minutes

1.   In the Initial Configuration Tasks window, click *Configure networking*. The Network Connections window displays.

2.   Right-click the *Local Area Connection* icon and choose *Properties*. The Local Area Connection Properties sheet displays.

3.   Select *Internet Protocol Version 4 (TCP/IPv4)* and click *Properties*. The Internet Protocol Version 4 (TCP/IPv4) Properties sheet displays.

4.   Select the *Use the following IP address* option and configure the following settings:

   - IP address: *10.10.0.31*
   - Subnet mask: *255.255.255.0*
   - Default gateway: Leave blank
   - Preferred DNS server: *10.10.0.31*
   - Alternate DNS server: Leave blank

5.   Click *OK* to accept your settings and close the Internet Protocol Version 4 (TCP/IPv4) Properties sheet.

6.   Click *Close* to close the Local Area Connection Properties sheet.

7.   Close the Network Connections window.

Adding Computers to a Domain

Overview	To add computers to a domain, perform the following steps.
Completion time	5 minutes

1.   Click *Start* > *Control Panel*. The Control Panel window displays.

2.   Click *System and Security* > *System*. The System control panel displays.

3.   Click *Change settings*. The System Properties sheet displays.

4.   Click *Change*. The Computer Name/Domain Changes dialog box displays.

5.   In the Computer name text box, type *StudentXX*

6.   Select the *Domain* option, type *contoso* in the text box, and then click *OK*. A Windows Security dialog box displays.

7.   Authenticate with the *Administrator* user name and the *Pa$$w0rd* password and then click *OK*. A message box displays, welcoming you to the domain.

8.   Click *OK*. Another message box displays, prompting you to restart the computer.

9.   Click *OK*.

10. Click *Close* to close the System Properties dialog box.

11. When prompted to restart your computer to apply these changes, click *Restart Now*. The computer restarts.

Installing the Remote Administration Tools for Windows	
Overview	To install the Remote Administration Tools for Windows, perform the following steps.
Completion time	5 minutes

1.   Click *Start*, right-click *Computer*, then and choose *Manage*.

2.   Select *Features*.

3.   Click *Add Features*.

4.   Select *Group Policy Management*.

5.   Expand *Remote Server Administration Tools*.

6.   Expand *Role Administration Tools*.

7.   Select *AD DS and AD LDS Tools*.

8.   Click *Install*.

9.   When the installation is complete, click *Close*.

10. If you are prompted to restart Windows now, click *Yes*.